FIVE
AND
TEN

The Fabulous Life of F. W. Woolworth

by

John K. Winkler

Specially revised by the author

Martino Publishing
Mansfield Centre, CT
2014

Martino Publishing
P.O. Box 373,
Mansfield Centre, CT 06250 USA

ISBN   978-1-61427-631-9

© *2014 Martino Publishing*

Cover design by T. Matarazzo

Printed in the United States of America On 100% Acid-Free Paper

FIVE AND TEN

The Fabulous Life of F. W. Woolworth

by

John K. Winkler

Specially revised by the author

a bantam *biography*

published by bantam books, inc., new york

FIVE AND TEN

A BANTAM BOOK
published by arrangement with the author.

BANTAM edition published October, 1957

This edition especially revised by the author, 1957

.

The author wishes to acknowledge the courtesy of the F. W. Woolworth Company in permitting unrestricted access to company records.

Contents

Chapter I

Nickels, Dimes and a Man

THIS is as much the biography of a business as of a man.

The man shaped the business; the business formed the man. Both were controlled and developed by the vast and colorful expansion of the United States during the eventful decades following the Civil War.

The man was Frank Winfield Woolworth, a dissatisfied hand on his father's farm in northern New York. The business was the Five-and-Ten-Cent Store.

The Five and Ten, as it is known today, has become as closely woven into the fabric of daily life as the radio and TV, the milkman, the newspaper. In the number of its customers, it rivals the movies.

The millions who daily go shopping and adventuring in these stores are not lured by advertising or other modern methods of salesmanship. They come because they know their every need can be satisfied quickly, conveniently—but most of all because of the sheer wonder of what their nickels and dimes will buy.

Half a century ago the Five and Ten consisted of a mere handful of shabby little shops scattered mostly through Pennsylvania. They dealt principally in pots and pans because other goods at this low price were

1

nonexistent. They were totally ignored by reputable merchants and looked down upon even by the small public which they served.

Then, peeping from behind the conservative skirts of the misnamed Gay Nineties, the Five and Ten, often referred to as the Dime Store, boldly asserted itself. It took advantage of new manufacturing processes and induced and cajoled manufacturers to sell their products through Five and Ten. Before long an astonishing variety of articles was to be found on its counters. Thus it extended the purchasing power of nickel and dime so amazingly as to revolutionize the equipment in the home, indeed the very appearance of the American people themselves.

Today there are thousands of Five and Ten stores in many lands.

Although it has increased its price range and become a direct competitor of the department store, Five and Ten's basic appeal remains the same—the wondrous purchasing power of the nickel and its companion, that thin tenth-part of the Great American Dollar.

All great ideas are simple and generally traceable to a tenacious, believing individual. So it was in this case.

Frank Woolworth clung to his belief in the future of the Five and Ten and won out over incredible obstacles.

This is his story—told largely in his own words.

Chapter II

A Poor Boy Makes a Slow Start

THE first twenty-one years of Frank Woolworth's life were passed on farms in Jefferson County, northern New York.

To the farm boy the coldest thing in the world was the handle of a pitchfork on a freezing winter morning.

In the North Country the winters were long; summers brief. Almost every morning from November to April a path had to be shoveled through the snow from the house to the barn. Then hay had to be pitched down to the cattle and the cows milked. It was the same hay which in late summer the farm boy had put away in the "peak" of the barn, amid broiling dust-laden atmosphere.

Frank and his younger brother, Charles Sumner, called Sum for short and the only other child in the family, had to get along with one pair of coarse cowhide boots a year. Charles S. Woolworth, who is still hale at eighty-three, recalls that along in April or early May, when he and Frank followed the harrow for days at a time, the seams in the heels of the worn boots would open up and let in a great deal of dirt which had to be shaken out at frequent intervals.

"I remember going after the cows at half past five

in the morning in late September when there was a white frost and we were barefoot," says the brother. "We would stand on the ground upon which the cows had been lying to get a little warmth into our nearly frozen feet. In late October we would pick up potatoes until our backs ached and our fingers were encrusted with dirt and numb with cold. No wonder we yearned to break away from the endless drudgery."

Escape, however, was difficult. For generations the Woolworths had tilled the soil, either as tenants or independent farmers, and the men of the family were trained to no other work.

The surname Woolworth is an American adaptation of an ancient English locality designation. As far back as the Thirteenth century there were Woley, Wolley and Wooley villages and parishes in various parts of England. The colonial progenitor of the family, Richard, a weaver, was known as Wolley as well as Woolworth in the early records of Newbury, Massachusetts, where he landed in 1678. Succeeding generation spread over New England and upper New York State, married local girls, reared families of generous proportions and acquired land. For the most part they were a frugal, industrious, God-fearing folk.

The early 1840's found the weaver's great-grandson, Jasper Woolworth, farming what was known as the old Moody place in the town of Rodman, Jefferson County, New York. He was aided by his son, John Hubbell Woolworth, born August 16, 1821.

On near-by Pillar Point—a peninsula extending into Lake Ontario—lived Henry McBrier, his wife, Kezia Sloan, and their eight children. The McBriers had come to America in 1825 from County Down, Ireland. Like the Woolworths, they were staunch Methodists.

One McBrier daughter, Fanny, attracted the eye of John Hubbell Woolworth, and the neighborhood agreed that John was a lucky fellow when the raven-haired, blue-eyed Fanny consented to become his bride. They were married January 14, 1851.

On Jasper Woolworth's farm, in addition to the main house, was a small cottage on a hill; and here John Woolworth took his twenty-year-old bride. He continued to manage his father's farm.

In this cottage on the hill the two Woolworth sons were born: Frank Winfield, April 13, 1852; and Charles Sumner, August 1, 1856. The latter was named for the eminent abolitionist Charles Sumner, whose anti-slavery views the Woolworths and McBriers shared. Frank Winfield, so far as can be learned, represented merely a pleasing "fancy" combination that appealed to the parents.

Late in 1858, Grandfather Woolworth sold his holdings in Rodman and John Woolworth had to find a new home for his wife and small sons. The following spring found them settled on a farm near Great Bend in the same county.

Great Bend—so-called because of a sweeping curve in the Black River at that point—was a hamlet of 125 souls which boasted a one-room stone schoolhouse, a general store and post office, and two churches—Methodist and Baptist. The surrounding country was rolling and beautiful, well-wooded and watered, and steeped in historic lore. For centuries various tribes of Indians—traveling the great water highway from the interior of North America to the Atlantic—fished and hunted, even farmed, along the near-by shores of Lake Ontario and the St. Lawrence River. Then came border and territorial wars between the British, the French and their various Indian allies; the war of the American Revolution; and finally the migration of permanent settlers, mostly Americans of pioneer New England stock, such as the Woolworths.

A colorful character in local history was Joseph Bonaparte, brother of Napoleon and one-time King of Spain, who in the early years of the century built a home for his mistress, Anne Savage, at the bend of Indian River only a few miles from Great Bend. On the doorposts was the Bonaparte coat of arms. A little further away was Lake Bonaparte, Ex-King Joe's hunting lodge, where he and his followers would float in a great Venetian gondola and fish and banquet and sing and dream of a new Napoleonic empire. They plotted to rescue Napoleon I from St. Helena and bring him to Cape Vincent, where they actually built a house for Napoleon's use—called the cup-and-saucer house because of its appearance.

Young Frankie Woolworth listened eagerly to these tales of past splendor, little dreaming that some day he himself would be surrounded with Napoleonic grandeur with an empire of his own creation.

Farmer John Woolworth, however, was concerned more with the problem of making a living than with tales of past glory. He was a fairly capable farmer but an impractical business man—an easy mark for schemers and often in financial straits. There was a mortgage of $1,600 on the new property, carrying interest at 7%, and twice a year $56 had to be raised. This was always an anxious time for the family and particularly for Fanny McBrier Woolworth, whose duty it was to begin saving for the next instalment the moment the current one was paid.

"We had no luxuries but we were not poverty-stricken," remarks Charles S. Woolworth. "We always had enough to eat but the struggle to make ends meet was never absent. We couldn't have gotten along if mother hadn't been a good manager. The farm consisted of 108 acres and we ran eight cows. Our principal crops were dairy products and potatoes. These had to be hauled by team to Watertown. Occasionally Father would take a load of wood in to the farmers' wood market in Watertown, but like as not his wood would be green, instead of well-dried out, and he'd have to stand around all day in the cold waiting for a buyer—then have to take a low price."

Watertown, the seat of Jefferson County and eleven miles from Great Bend, was a thriving community of some 7,000 or 8,000 inhabitants. Its public square, encircled by a wooden sidewalk, was the center of the county's activities. Around the square were located the drygoods, hardware and grocery stores, the blacksmith, the bank, the undertaker and so on. Here farmers of Jefferson County like the Woolworths brought their vegetables and wood to sell. On market days the place was crowded with their teams and pungs piled high with produce; and noisy with their gossip and barterings. Here also came the ladies of Watertown in their hoop skirts and bonnets, often accompanied by a younger son who carried the shopping basket. On holidays the square became a social center, a band playing in the little round white bandstand.

But the Woolworths knew no holidays. On the farm even Sunday was only a partial day of rest. The Methodist Church down the pike was the family's chief social outlet. John Woolworth and his wife both sang in the choir; while Frank and Sumner, brushed and scrubbed, attended Sunday school.

Frank had been sent to the red schoolhouse at Rodman and continued his schooling at Great Bend, where the terms were short. In Marietta, Ohio, lives a woman of ninety-seven, Emma Penniman Otis, who was young Woolworth's teacher at Great Bend. Her faculties are unimparied and her memory good. "Frankie Woolworth was a bright pupil and never gave me the least trouble," she says. "He was inclined to be sober-minded, not at all prankish and always had his lessons. He was a good-looking boy and pleasant in disposition.

"In those days," Mrs. Otis recalls, "it was the custom for teachers to board around and some places were not so pleasant. Mrs. Woolworth invited me to remain at her home longer than I was supposed to stay and I appreciated this kindness. Indeed, Mrs. Woolworth was always doing kind things for others. She was a good housekeeper and made everyone feel at home."

Frank Woolworth grew up tall, thin, not overly robust. He was, however, quick, nimble-witted and persistent in whatever he undertook. Distinctly he had an eye for decorative effects. He replaced the rickety old rail fence on both sides of the road in front of the house with a neat picket one, the timber for which he hewed himself. And he beautified the farmhouse yard with saplings transplanted from a near-by forest. One, a great maple, still lives.

The boy's proudest possession at this time was a flute. This was the first of many instruments upon which he attempted to express himself. Though music remained a life-long passion, he was never able to master any instrument or to carry a tune.

Sometimes Frank would accompany his father to Watertown and haunt the roundhouse of the Rome, Watertown & Ogdensburg Railroad. It was the era of railroad building, and as small communities became linked with the outside world every imagination, young and old, was filled with the thrilling possibilities of the new method of transportation. On one proud day an engineer beckoned Frank to a ride in one of the locomotives with its wide, flaring steam stack, and for months the lad dreamed of becoming a railroad man. If there had been the slightest opportunity for him in this direction, the course of his life would have been altered.

Strangely enough, though the Civil War was raging during his most impressionable years, the boy had no yearning for military glory. Keen abolitionists and Lincoln supporters as they were, to many people of the North Country the bloody battlefields of Virginia and elsewhere seemed remote. Yet Frank always remembered the thrill of exultation that greeted Lee's surrender; and the numb horror that swept the country-side when Lincoln was assassinated.

At sixteen Woolworth's schooling was over and he had to put in full time on the farm. More than ever he grew to detest the rough, monotonous farm work. More than ever he became determined to break away from it. His mother, a staunch ally, scraped up enough money for him to take two brief courses in a Watertown commercial college. When these were completed Woolworth set out to find a job. The highest post at which he could aim was to get behind the counter of some store.

Harnessing the family mare to a cutter, for the ground was deep in snow, he drove to Cathage, a town of some 1,500 people, four miles east of Great Bend. Carthage contained a cluster of stores, including a furniture and undertaking shop and a meat market.

Young Woolworth called at each shop, eagerly asking for work. But no one wanted the tall country lad and he returned home, deeply discouraged.

The truth is, though the young job seeker but dimly realized it, he was a victim of times that were out of joint. Financial and mercantile interests were still feeling the terrific strain of the war years. A gold dollar was worth $1.50 to $2 in paper money. Prices and the cost of living were sky-high. Few women could afford to pay twenty-five cents a yard for ordinary print calico or forty cents a yard for unbleached muslin. The result was stagnant trade.

Finally, Daniel McNeil, who ran the small general store at Great Bend, told Woolworth he could help him out on rush days but he couldn't afford to pay him any wages. Woolworth accepted the offer gratefully in order to gain experience.

Matters, however, came to a head in March, 1873, when his uncle, Albon S. McBrier, offered him $18 a month with board and lodgings to work on his farm. The time had come when Frank must shift for himself, with financial results. He was nearing twenty-one. His younger brother was now old enough to take his place on the farm.

There was a family conference. The job with the uncle was definite and certain. His father did not think Frank should refuse it. Yet the very thought of farm work filled the youth with such a loathing that he begged for a little more time before making a decision. Fanny Woolworth, as usual, pleaded her son's cause. He was not robust and she longed to see him in some more protected field. They won a brief respite.

Frank explained the situation to McNeil. The kindly storekeeper, appreciative of the lad's services, promised to do what he could for him when he went into Watertown to buy his goods.

These were anxious days. Woolworth waited at McNeil's house every time McNeil went to Watertown to learn the result. Finally, one night he was rewarded.

"Say," exclaimed McNeil, "there's an opening at Augsbury and Moore's! Heard about it today. I know Augsbury. I'll give you a letter to him."

Augsbury & Moore, located on what was known as the American Corner of the public square, was one of the leading drygoods stores in Watertown. A chance with them represented the very height of Woolworth's ambition.

Early the next morning Woolworth appeared at the store, only to be told that Mr. Augsbury was at home, ill. He asked where Augsbury lived and found his way there.

"So you want a job?" asked Augsbury after reading McNeil's letter and taking in at a glance his visitor's farm shirt, cowhide boots and the thick home-knit scarf which he wore in lieu of an overcoat. "Do you drink? Do you smoke? What do you do that's bad?"

The country boy replied that he didn't drink nor smoke and that he wasn't conscious of doing anything that was very bad.

"Well, you look too green to me; you've had no experience," said Augsbury. "But I'll tell you what to do. Go down and see Mr. Moore—if he wants to give you a trial it's all right with me."

William H. Moore, though but a dozen years Woolworth's senior, was an imposing figure to the lanky youth in homespun. He wore his side-whiskers and fashionable skirted coat with satin-faced lapels with an air of authority. Sitting behind his slant-topped desk on a raised platform, he promptly put the young applicant through an examination which made the latter's head spin. Why did he want to leave the farm? Didn't he know that store hours were longer and the work not so healthy? What did he know about clerking anyway? Finally, Moore said: "If we take you on, you'll have to do all the mean work in the store, deliver packages, wash windows, get down early and sweep the floor, do all the cleaning and any other dirty work that needs to be done. It will be the hardest work you ever did in your life."

"I guess I can do it, sir," replied Woolworth. "What are you going to pay me?"

The question seemed to shock Moore.

"Pay you?" he exclaimed. "Why, you ought to pay us for teaching you the business! When you go to school you have to pay fees. Well, we won't charge you any tuition fee but you'll have to work for nothing until we can decide if you are worth anything and how much."

Woolworth's heart sank.

"How long would I have to work for nothing?" he asked.

"At least six months," replied Moore in a tone of finality.

Woolworth thought fast, then proposed a compromise. He told Moore that by dint of odd jobs and other labor he had saved $50. This he calculated would pay his board and lodgings in Watertown for three months.

"I'll work the first three months for nothing," he said, "if you will pay me $3.50 a week for the second three months."

After considerable discussion this proposal was accepted, and it was agreed that the new apprentice should report for work the following Monday, March 24, 1873. He asked if he could be at bit late because his father was bringing in a load of potatoes and by coming in with the potatoes he could save thirty-three cents railroad fare. Then the young man drove home, exultant, to break the news.

On the appointed morning the Woolworths, father and son, started before dawn for Watertown. Frank's modest bundle of clothing nestled amid the barrels of potatoes. In his hand he carried his precious flute. Fanny McBrier Woolworth's eyes filled with tears; Brother Sum stood in the doorway beside her, a lantern in his hand. They waved as long as the sleigh was in sight, shouting "Good-by, Frankie, good-by." Great Bend was just waking up. At Dan McNeil's general store a smoked-up lantern was making a pumpkin-sized hole of yellow light in the darkness.

The snow was heavy and it was midmorning before the steaming horses pulled their heavy load into Water-town. Frank waved his arms for warmth, shook the stiffness out of his limbs and crossed the square at a lope toward his new employment.

Woolworth never forgot the trials and tribulations of his first day with Augsbury & Moore. Years later he recounted them to B. C. Forbes, the financial writer, who recorded them thus in his meaty book, *Men Who Are Making America:*

Mr. Augsbury was the first one I encountered. "Bub, don't they wear any collars in your neighborhood?" was how he greeted me. I replied: "No." "No neckties either?" I again replied: "No." "Is this old flannel shirt the best you have to wear?" he next asked. "Yes, sir," I replied. "Well, you'd better go out and get a white shirt and a collar and a tie before you begin work."

I went and got properly rigged up, and shortly after I got back to the store Mr. Augsbury went to lunch. Nobody told me what to do. I hung around, feeling foolish, waiting for something to do. The clerks stared at me and sneered at me— I was a boob from the country accustomed to wearing nothing but old flannel shirts without collar or tie. At least, I imagined that was what they were thinking—and they afterward told me that that was exactly their sizing up of me. When most of the clerks had gone to dinner—lunch, as we call it nowadays—in came an old farmer and said to me: "Young man, I want a spool of thread." I didn't know where they kept the thread, so I

went over to Mr. Moore, who was busy at his
desk, and asked him. "Right in front of your nose,
young man," he snapped without looking up from
his writing. I pulled out a drawer directly in front
of me and, sure enough, found it full of spools of
thread. "I want number forty," said the farmer. I
never knew till that moment that thread had a
number. I fumbled all around the drawer looking
for number 40, but could not find it. I appealed to
Mr. Moore to know if we kept number 40. "Certainly; right in the drawer in front of you," he said
quite sharply. I had to tell him: "I can't find any."
"Just as I expected," he said testily as he got down
from his desk and showed me the right kind of
thread. He immediately returned to his desk.

"How much is it, young man?" asked the farmer.
I had to turn once more to Mr. Moore. It was
eight cents. The farmer pulled out a ten-cent
shinplaster. "Mr. Moore, where do I get change?"
I had to ask. "Come right up to the desk and make
out a ticket," he ordered me. I picked up one of
the blanks and studied it all over to see what I
could do with it. But I was stumped. "Mr. Moore,
I don't believe I know how to make this out," I
had to confess. "Hand it to me; I will show you,"
he replied. Next I had to ask: "Where do I get
my change?" "There's the cashier right there;
can't you see him?" he said impatiently.

No sooner had the farmer gone out than another
came in with the request: "I want a pair of mittens." "Mr. Moore, have we got any mittens?" I
had to ask. "Hanging right up in front of your
nose, young man," was his reply. And there they
were, although I hadn't noticed them. The farmer,
after a lot of fingering and trying on, selected an
old-fashioned, homemade woolen pair. "How

much?" he asked. I told him I didn't know but I called over to Mr. Moore: "How much are these mittens?" Mr. Moore by this time had had about enough of my interruptions. He replied impatiently: "Look at the ticket; can't you see the ticket on there?" The ticket said 25 cents and in payment the farmer pulled out a dollar bill.

This time I knew how to make out a check and where to get change, so that I finished the transaction without bothering Mr. Moore any more. I also learned where to find the price ticket on merchandise. I was keeping my eyes open as best I could.

The next morning the new man started the day early: sweeping out the store, dusting, cleaning the cuspidors, performing other menial tasks. Then he was given packages to deliver. Only at the noon dinner hour did he get a chance to wait on customers. Later in the week Minor Merrill, supervisor of Woolworth's home township, came into the store and asked to be personally waited on by Frank. Merrill wanted ten yards of calico for his wife. Young Woolworth stepped behind the drygoods counter with pretended confidence and reached for a bolt of cloth. Having no more idea than the man in the moon how to measure off ten yards of material, he bravely began to unroll the bolt. Soon there was a cascade of calico flowing over the counter and onto the floor in a hopeless mess. Proprietor Moore looked up from his books, uttered one agonized word: "Stop!" and marched down to wait upon the customer himself.

Then, one afternoon about four, Moore remarked casually without raising his eyes from his books: "Woolworth, take all of the goods out of the front window and wash it good." As Woolworth started off he called after him, still without raising his eyes: "When you've done that—trim it over."

Woolworth's blue eyes shone. This was *real* store work. Midnight found him still at work. Helping himself to remnants of fabric, mostly red in color, and other wares from stock, he shifted them from one position to another hundreds of times before they pleased his eye. The next morning Mr. Moore stopped outside the window for a long minute while Woolworth tarried with his broom. According to his custom, Moore said nothing when pleased and he said nothing now. But from then on it was part of Woolworth's job to dress the windows of Augsbury & Moore.

Soon he made himself useful in the stock room, too, where he was quick to learn the names and grades of materials. Woolworth also found friends in the store who helped him over many a rough spot. One was E. W. Barrett, the head clerk, who was earning the tremendous salary of $13 a week. Another was Mrs. A. E. Coons, a stout, matronly woman clerk. Her kindnesses Woolworth never forgot and he was able later to show his appreciation in a substantial manner.

Thus, despite setbacks, the country youth was able to hold on to his first job for two and a half years. He got his $3.50 at the end of three months; was raised to $4 in six months, $4.50 in a year and finally to $6 a week. With a salary of a dollar for each working day he felt like a nabob. He had long since discarded his mother's big woollen scarf for an overcoat. Now he brought himself a high plug hat and displayed it for the first time at church on Easter morning.

No one in Watertown was more pleased with himself than Frank Woolworth. At his boarding house, though, other lodgers were having some fun at his expense. Despairing of his ability to master the flute, the young clerk now possessed himself of a violin. He practiced on it industriously; but in spite of his earnestness, the musical effect was far from harmonious. Many of the boarders prayed to heaven he would return to the flute because its tones, at least, were less exacerbating. But Frank persisted, as in everything he undertook. However, in music he never won out; for the truth of the matter was that he possessed no sense of pitch and was never able to carry a tune.

"No one thought Woolworth would rise higher than a clerkship," recalled the late Supreme Court Justice Edgar C. Emerson. "We were young men together and boarded at the same place. Sundays we would frequently visit friends on Pillar Point and Woolworth would do his best to make music with that fiddle. Maybe because of that, people who knew him in his early Watertown days never thought he'd ever amount to anything."

There wasn't much opportunity for diversion, however, for the young clerk in "The Corner" store of Augsbury & Moore, whose hours were from seven in the morning until nine at night, six days a week. The confinement began to tell. He grew pale and thin.

At the beginning of Woolworth's third year in harness a young man named Perry R. Smith bought Mr. Augsbury's interest in the store and the firm became Moore & Smith. After sizing up the help Proprietor Smith agreed with his partner that clerk Woolworth, though a bust as a salesman, *was* good at cataloguing merchandise and arranging displays. By now this was also clerk Woolworth's opinion of clerk Woolworth— he felt he was worth higher wages.

In the fall of 1875, head clerk E. W. Barrett and his friend Golding, senior clerk with the rival dry-goods store of A. Bushnell & Company, left Watertown to open a 99-cent store in Port Huron, Michigan. Woolworth, hearing of the Bushnell vacancy, promptly

went in to apply for the job. At first glance, he noticed
the disorder of the counters and visioned how attractive
he could make them. Accordingly, when Mr. Bushnell
asked him what salary he wanted, Woolworth blurted
out: "I think I am worth ten dollars a week, sir." And
to his amazement he heard Bushnell reply: "That
will be satisfactory." Moore & Smith were equally
astonished and made no attempt to meet the rival
terms. So Woolworth went to work in Bushnell's.

One of the requirements of the new job was that he
sleep in the cellar to protect the store from burglars.
He was given a revolver and a companion in the
person of Harry Moody, the seventeen-year-old check
boy. Harry was a gay, jolly lad and he and Woolworth
became firm friends. Neither dreamed, as they lay
on their cots in the dark basement listening for mar-
auders, that eventually they would be associated in a
$65,000,000 enterprise.

Disillusionment with his new environment came
swiftly to Woolworth. Bushnell, conservative and un-
imaginative, discouraged all his efforts to dress the
windows and tone up the counters. Bushnell wanted
not a decorator but a salesman—and salesmanship was
still Woolworth's weak point. One day the merchant
led his new clerk into the basement and told him
bluntly that he could no longer pay him $10 a week.

"Why," said Bushnell, "I have boys earning six
dollars a week who sell more goods than you. I'll have
to reduce your salary to eight dollars."

Woolworth accepted the cut without demur but
became more and more depressed. He wrote a sad
letter to his mother who responded with a message of
encouragement, ending with this assurance: "Some
day, my son, you will be a rich man."

Though he plugged away as hard as ever, he grew

thinner and paler. Finally his health broke down completely.

The doctor said he was too ill to work and ordered him back to the farm to recuperate. Carson Peck, a young school teacher, was given his place at the store temporarily because it was believed his recovery would be rapid.

However, as the months passed and Frank lay in a state of complete mental and physical exhaustion on the farm, he became despondent. The chance of a mercantile career seemed lost forever.

Chapter III

Romance

SLEEPING in Bushnell's basement, long hours of sedentary toil, and boarding-house food were undoubtedly physical factors in Frank Woolworth's collapse. But another factor also played its part, both in the young man's breakdown and in his recovery: Frank Woolworth was in love.

While working for Moore & Smith he had met a lonely young Canadian girl named Jennie Creighton, who had recently come to Watertown to earn her living with her needle. Though she resided with a cousin, Miss Margaret Morrison, in the old Pierce homestead on lower Franklin street, she was often homesick for her eight younger brothers and sisters who lived with her widowed father, Thomas H. Creighton, across the border in Picton, Ontario. The Creightons were of Irish and English extraction. Their circumstances were, if anything, even more humble than those of the Woolworths.

Fair of face, with blond hair and blue eyes, Jennie was sympathetic and understanding, the sort of girl to whom a young man could bring his hopes, his ambitions and his troubles. The more Woolworth saw of her the more determined he became to win her for his wife. This determination had greatly influenced his bold demand upon Mr. Bushnell for the $10-a-week salary.

Upon landing the new job, he had promptly proposed to the comely young seamstress and been accepted. Their hopes had soared skyward with all they could do on $10 a week. Then when it became apparent that he and Bushnell would never agree, he became panic-stricken: if he lost this job he would lose everything—including Jennie.

But he didn't lose Jennie. During his long illness she was a faithful and cheering visitor to the Woolworth farm. As spring brought new strength to the invalid, he again began to plan for the future. His mercantile days he believed were ended; but would Miss Creighton become a farmer's wife? She would. And so, June 11, 1876, they were married in the parlor of the Woolworth home. The young couple were literally penniless.

However, the groom found a four-acre farm priced at $900; and after signing a note for $300 and taking out a mortgage for $600, he and Jennie moved in. Here they raised chickens, potatoes—anything they could sell. The experience gave Woolworth a distaste for chicken in any form for the rest of his life. They managed to live, little more.

Things were going none too well four months later when a letter from W. H. Moore summoned Woolworth to Watertown. Moore had learned that "dressing up" the windows was good for business. He now offered the young farmer $10 a week to return to his old job.

Woolworth said he would have to consult his wife before accepting the offer. Long and earnestly he and Jennie Woolworth discussed the problem of what they could do with the farm and the chickens; and finally

Jennie solved the problem in her own capable way.

"Frank, you go back to the store," she said, "and I'll stay here and take care of the chickens until we get a chance to sell."

It was a courageous decision for a young woman— she was but twenty-two—who had never before lived alone on a farm. But she insisted and the following Monday found Woolworth back at the counter and living in the old Watertown boarding house. Each Saturday fortnight, he came home to spend Sunday. Thus almost a year passed. Jennie Woolworth never complained.

However, in the fall of '77, a neighbor offered to trade a second-hand sewing machine for the chickens and the Woolworths seized the opportunity. Jennie was expecting a baby. They rented the farm and moved their few possessions into a one-story wing attached to a two-story frame dwelling at 236-8 Franklin street in Watertown, and wondered if such bliss could last.

In the middle of the winter word came that Woolworth's mother was ill. He and Jennie rushed to Great Bend as fast as a livery-stable sleigh could take them, and were at her side when she died February 15, 1878. She was but forty-seven.

After her death, Woolworth's father and the younger brother, Sumner, were quite lost. Sumner was as anxious as Frank had been to break away from the farm; and Frank, whose influence with Moore & Smith was steadily growing, persuaded the firm to make a place for his brother. A housekeeper was hired to look after the father.

Saturday nights now often found three Woolworths back of the counter in Moore & Smith's, for Jennie sometimes helped out when trade was brisk. Thus, despite their extra expenses, the frugal Woolworths

managed that year to save fifty dollars and to con-
tribute a like amount to Woolworth's father.

However, in the late spring of 1878, business wasn't
so brisk and as the warmer days brought no added
trade Woolworth was forced to take a cut in salary
from $10 to $8.50 a week. This was a major catastrophe
to the young couple on Franklin Street, for their first
child, Helena, was born a few weeks later.

It was during this dark period that a seemingly
casual episode occurred that was to have a profound
effect upon the young clerk's future. One day when
business was slacker than usual, a young man with an
air of prosperity in his manner and appearance entered the store. This was none other than Golding,
the former Bushnell clerk, whom Woolworth had replaced when Golding left Watertown with Moore &
Smith's head clerk, E. W. Barrett, to open a 99-cent
store of their own in the West.

"How's business, Mr. Moore?" asked Golding, who
had come East on a combined business and pleasure
trip.

"Slow," replied the merchant, "very slow. In fact,
I've seldom seen it worse in the last twenty years."

"I am sorry to hear that," remarked Golding. "Why
don't you make trade by running special cut-rate bargains?"

"Cut-rate bargains?" asked Moore. "What kind of
store business is that?"

"Why, do you mean to say you have never heard of
the five-cent counter?"

Moore said he hadn't, and Golding told him a curi-
ous story:

A season or two previous, it seemed, a New York
jobbing firm, Spelman Brothers, found itself over-
stocked with handkerchiefs manufactured to sell at
the standard price of twenty-five cents each. Into their

office walked a hustling young road salesman named Bennett with the bright idea that he could get rid of the superfluous stock if the jobbers would consider selling the handkerchiefs for five cents each. Spelman Brothers agreed. Elated, Bennett returned to his home territory, Michigan, where he offered his bargain to leading merchants. Much to his surprise the store-keepers shied away. The customary price for hand-kerchiefs had long been twenty-five cents; therefore they became suspicious of the quality of any offered below that figure. However, one merchant finally agreed to sponsor a sale, provided Bennett would assume all risks and take back any handkerchiefs that remained unsold. The sale was a complete success. Not only were the handkerchief counters quickly cleared, but the customers purchased other goods as well. Thereafter canny merchants in that section had lured their customers with five-cent sales.

Golding added that he and Barrett often ran a five-cent sale. In fact, on his present trip he was stopping off in New York at Spelman Brothers, who now carried a special wholesale line in five-cent merchandise.

"Why don't you try a five-cent counter in Watertown?" he asked.

"Perhaps I shall," responded Moore slowly, but without any particular enthusiasm.

Listening with all ears to this colloquy was Frank Woolworth. But he said nothing. The incident passed. Business grew worse.

Moore said nothing either, but in August, on his customary buying trip to New York, he went to Spelman Brothers and ordered a hundred dollars worth of five-cent goods. These included steel pens, crocheting needles, buttonhooks, watch keys, combs, book straps, safety pins, collar buttons, pencils, baby bibs, tin pans, washbasins and dippers, turkey-red napkins, thimbles, soap, stationery, harmonicas.

The goods arrived a week before the county fair. It was Woolworth's task to arrange the display.

In the rear of the store were some old sewing tables, about five feet long and two feet wide. On two of these Woolworth improvised a counter, running down the center aisle, over which he posted a large placard reading:

ANY ARTICLE ON THIS COUNTER FIVE CENTS

The sale took place the opening day of the fair.

As things turned out, it was just about the greatest day in the life of Frank Woolworth. The square was crowded with people in holiday spirit. Most of them had a little money to spend—not much, but a little. Word quickly spread of the five-cent goods at Moore & Smith's. It was more exciting news than whose sow or mare had won a prize, because it affected every one of them—and that bargain urge which had lain dormant in them all.

By nightfall the five-cent counter was bare and customers stood around asking for more nickel goods. Moore wrote a telegram to Spelman Brothers, asking for the rush shipment of a duplicate order. Woolworth was exhausted, but so excited he didn't know he was tired. It was he who ran up the three flights of stairs to the Western Union office, located in the same building as the store, with Moore's telegram.

Years afterward Mrs. Coons, the saleslady who had befriended Woolworth from the beginning, used to laugh when she told how they could all hear Frank pounding up those stairs that night, two at a time.

Other upstate merchants copied the idea. The five-cent counter became a craze. Even individuals were attracted to this new form of merchandising. One man bought fifty dollars' worth of five-cent goods, carried his stock to Adams Center and placed it on sale in his barn. Within three days he was back for more.

Many who are alive today in Watertown remember the excitement. Moore & Smith became a wholesale as well as a retail five-cent outlet. Moore believed five-cent goods might be sold successfully in stores devoted to such goods alone. Many believed with him—and no one more firmly than clerk Woolworth.

Soon, however, there were signs that the boom of the nickel counter was on the wane. The goods were cheap and shoddy and lacked variety. Profits were meager without sales in large volume. Experienced observers scoffed at the whole business as a passing fad.

Frank Woolworth disagreed. He centered his ambitions toward one definite aim—to open a five-cent store *of his own.*

He went to Mr. Moore and asked him how much he'd need to open a five-cent store. Moore said it could be done for three hundred dollars. That seemed a mountainous amount but Woolworth set out to raise it. His uncle McBrier, the only "capitalist" in the family, told him the idea was stuff and nonsense, that he'd better hold on to his job, that he (McBrier) would as soon throw money in the river as put it in this crazy, newfangled business.

But Woolworth's determination would not down.

He turned again to Moore and asked him diffidently if Moore & Smith would give him credit for $300 worth of goods, taking only his note as security. Moore, who had grown to respect Woolworth's tenacity, said the firm would.

So, on a bitterly cold day in late January, 1879, Frank Woolworth started out on a new tack, but upon the same quest, which had brought him from the farm six years before—a foothold in the commercial world.

Chapter IV

Barnstorming with Pots and Pans

WHEN Woolworth started out to open a store of his own, the five-cent craze was definitely on the decline.

People now regarded the five-cent merchant as a fly-by-night adventurer, blood brother to the county fair con man and the Yankee pack peddler whose chicanery and sharp practices were notorious. Established merchants looked down on him.

Woolworth was well aware of the prejudice. He knew, too, that towns in Jefferson and adjoining counties of the North Country had been thoroughly exploited. But one thing he could not get out of his head —never could get out of his head—and that was that the five-cent store was not a mere fad but an idea with future possibilities. In new territory he believed he could prove it. So he struck out downstate and scouted a number of places between Watertown and Rome. None appealed to him and he moved on to Utica. To his surprise he found that this city of 35,000 people had been untouched by the five-cent idea, and here he determined to locate.

For hours he tramped the streets of downtown Utica, looking for a vacancy. Finally, in Bleecker street, near the busy corner of Genesee, he came upon a "to let"

sign over a small room. It fronted 13 feet on the street
and was 20 feet deep. For a long time the young merchant in embryo stood in the snow and slush and
pondered possibilities. Then he sought out the landlord, who inquired:

"What sort of store do you figure on opening, young
fellow?"

"Oh, I am going to sell notions and general merchandise," glibly replied Woolworth, on guard against
identifying himself with the despised five-centers.

"Wa'all, guess that's all right," allowed the owner.
"The rent will be thirty-five dollars a month, paid in
advance, and you'll have to sign a lease for a year."

That was a poser, and Woolworth talked long and
earnestly for more favorable terms. The landlord at
last agreed to waive the requirement of a year's lease
and to accept the initial instalment of the rent some-
time before the end of the first month. How and why
he won these concessions Woolworth was never afterward able to remember. But he did remember, even
after renting the small store, shaking in his boots and
hesitating for hours before sending a telegram to his
backer, Moore, asking the merchant to set aside certain goods for him.

"That telegram seemed to mean a definite casting of
the die," explained Woolworth years later. "I kept it in
my pocket and walked past the telegraph office many
times before summoning courage to send it. I didn't
wire my wife because I wanted to tell her myself."

However, he forgot the cold and his fatigue as he
sat by the stove in the railroad train on his way back
to Watertown; and he was in high spirits by the time
he reached home.

After breaking the news to his wife, who was as
elated as he, Woolworth hastened to Moore & Smith
to select his stock. The bill was $315.41, for which

Moore & Smith, as previously agreed, took his note. Woolworth helped pack the goods and label the crates; then he hurried back to Utica to get the store ready.

He scrubbed and cleared the place himself, bought plain pine boards and had counters made at a total cost of eight dollars. Other items were listed in his ledger:

Kerosene lamp	$5.50
Mallet	.38
Broom	.10
Kerosene oil can	.10
Hatchet	.75
Box opener	.25
Cash drawer	.50
Red cambric for front of counters	.53
Writing desk	1.55
Feather duster	.15
Office stool	.65
Total	$10.46

It is interesting to note that even in this first store Woolworth used red—a color he never abandoned.

The daybook, cashbook and ledger each cost sixty cents. Twenty and one-half pounds of wrapping paper at eight cents a pound came to $1.64. Freight charges for his crates of goods from Watertown amounted to $7.43. Another item of expense was $7.50 for 2,000 handbills, enumerating the items he would sell, and announcing his "Grand Opening" for eight o'clock on the evening of Saturday, February 22, 1879. He hired a boy to distribute these about the city.

The young merchant's capital was fast fading, but he gambled three dollars on a sign reading: "The

Great Five Cent Store." When the sign had been painted he looked at it ecstatically. The phrase was entirely his own. It illustrated his flair for showmanship and his advertising instinct.

The detailed records of the Utica venture, in the proprietor's own writing, are still in existence. They were exhumed by Woolworth shortly before his death for use in an autobiography which he planned in collaboration with Edward Mott Woolley. Unfortunately the work had only gotten under way when Woolworth died. Under the editorship of Mr. Woolley a fragment of the autobiography appeared in the old *McClure's Magazine.*

Here Woolworth listed the chief items in his stock, together with the price paid for each at wholesale. The figures show how thin was his margin of profit and how limited the nature of goods then available at five cents. The list and wholesale price per gross:

Toy dustpans	$4.75
Tin pepper boxes	3.75
Drinking cups	3.50
Gravy strainers	5.50
Tin scoops	5.65
Purses	5.25
Biscuit cutters	3.00
Flour dredges	5.25
School straps	4.50
Skimmers	2.50
Egg whips	5.50
Apple corers	5.75
Cast-iron and sad-iron stands	5.00
Fire shovels	5.50
Boot blacking	5.75
Animal soap	5.85
Stamped-in cup	5.50

Candlesticks	4.50	
Ladles	4.50	
A B C plates	2.50	
Scalloped pie plates	5.75	
Baseballs	4.75	
Cast-iron cover lifters	4.00	
Tack hammers	4.85	
Tack claws	5.25	
Animal cake cutters	4.00	
Cake turners	5.65	
Large graters	5.25	
Jelly-cake tins	4.75	
Writing books	5.00	
Pencil charms	5.75	
Lather brushes	5.50	
Tin spoons	4.00	
Police whistle	5.00	
Pie plates	4.75	
Red jewelry	5.00	
Turkey-red napkins	.50	per dozen
Hemstitched handkerchiefs	.40	” ”
Linen thread	.39	” ”
Barbers' thread	.43	” ”

Novelties, $1.15 to $1.40 per
    thousand

In the light of later mass production, these prices seem ridiculously high. For instance, pie plates for which the Great Five Cent Store had to pay $5.75 a gross, could be purchased in a few years for $3, then $2 a gross. Turkey-red napkins dropped to thirty and twenty cents a dozen; and the same story was true of pins, lead pencils and many other articles.

To give color to his counters, Woolworth had invested heavily ($10) in red jewelry. It seemed a daring move, yet these baubles, made of a sour-milk composition, had proved very popular with women in other five-cent stores.

"I began to unpack my goods on Wednesday or Thursday preceding the Saturday set for the opening," recalled Woolworth in his uncompleted autobiography. "And I worked like a Trojan. On Friday evening I had the goods all in the store, but everything was in a great litter, with loose paper scattered about on the floor and the goods in a general mix-up on the counters and shelves. To keep people from satisfying their curiosity and thus anticipating the grand opening, I had fastened paper at the doors and windows. While I was working in the muss, about nine o'clock, somebody knocked at the door. I went to see who it was, and found a woman standing there. She said she would like to come in and buy some goods.

" 'But the store isn't open for business, Madam,' I said. 'If you will come here tomorrow night things will be in shape and you can select what you want.'

" 'I know what I want,' she answered. 'I have read your circulars and I find among the list of goods a fire shovel at five cents. I wish to purchase a fire shovel.'

" 'Very well,' said I. 'Just step inside and I'll wrap it up for you.'

"She did so, and I sold her the shovel, which she carried away in triumph a minute later.

"She was my first customer and had I dreamed of the things that were destined to happen to me in subsequent years I most certainly should have taken her name, and kept that first money. As it is, I don't know who she was."

The Great Five Cent Store opened promptly at eight o'clock the next evening and the proprietor, freshly combed and washed, stood in the tiny doorway welcoming customers. He was not overwhelmed by the rush. In fact, the Grand Opening did not seem to create a single additional bubble of excitement in the tempo of Utica's Saturday night life. However, at midnight, when Woolworth counted up his shin-plasters (there was no metal five-cent coin in those days) he found that his receipts totaled an even nine dollars.

Monday's business was a good deal better—$41.22. Woolworth felt sufficiently encouraged to advertise for a clerk and invest ten cents in a money bag. Two days later he opened a bank account. On March 4 he sent Moore & Smith a one-hundred-dollar payment on his note. He hired two clerks, a young man named Edwins and a young lady named Stebbins, and arranged for an extra part-time salesman to come in Saturday nights.

For a fortnight trade boomed. One Sunday, in mid-March, Proprietor Woolworth marched gaily into the small Franklin street living room in Watertown and proudly presented his wife with a $45 fur dolman. It was his first display of extravagance, for he was rigorously holding his own living expenses to five dollars a week. Jennie Woolworth was overwhelmed by the gift and buoyantly they discussed plans for renting rooms, or even a whole house, in Utica.

Then, without warning, business slackened. Customers, curiosity abating, returned to their regular merchants, whose prices were higher but whose stock was much more diversified. In desperation Woolworth hired a boy to lug a sign about the streets and distributed several thousand handbills. These devices brought a renewed flurry of trade and Woolworth cautiously risked an order for more goods. Soon, however, the decline set in again. Each day in late April sales grew more meager, and in May a worried Woolworth realized that the jig was up. His first venture was a failure.

It soon would be a question of either closing his little store or having creditors do it for him.

The latter alternative was intolerable. He would close the store himself. But then—what next? Should he return to Watertown, tail between his legs, and beg back his old job of Moore & Smith? Or should he struggle on with his pet ambition to become an independent merchant?

It was a tough problem for a young man of twenty-seven, in debt and with a wife and child to look after. He pondered the situation during many a wakeful night in his Utica boarding house. Upon his decision depended his whole future and that of his little family.

The more he thought, the more he became convinced that his failure in Utica was due not to himself or to his idea, but mainly due to the poor location of his store and Utica itself, where trading was generally slack at the time. However, he did see one handicap in the five-cent idea—merchandise to sell at that figure was extremely limited. If he could increase the figure to ten cents the range would be much wider. Surely there were other communities that would appreciate inexpensive goods. If he could find one, he would choose his location more carefully and he was certain he would succeed. And find such a town he would, before resigning himself to clerking for some other man for the rest of his life.

Accordingly, on May 28, he drew $30 from the bank and set out on another scouting expedition. This trip had a more direct objective than his journey of four months before. For a friend in whom he had confidence had given such a glowing account of Lancaster, Pennsylvania, a live, growing city inhabited largely by thrifty Pennsylvania Dutch, that he determined to survey that city at once.

It was an all-day trip. The railroad fare alone was more than $10 each way, so Woolworth had to husband his resources. He ate sparingly and left his seat only when necessary to change cars.

So hurried was his passage through New York that this, his first view of the city, was blurred. About all he could remember was the Grand Central station at Forty-second Street and Fourth (now Park) Avenue with its great rounded dome, built in 1871 by Commodore Vanderbilt's New York Central system and the New Haven road; and the broad, boxlike cars, with their platforms only a foot or so above the rails, that seemed to pour endlessly into the great terminus.

"I reached Lancaster about dusk on a train from Philadelphia," recalled Woolworth forty years later. "As it happened, this was the very best time I could have arrived, for I saw Lancaster when it was at its best for my purpose. I was amazed as I walked up from the depot to see the crowds on the streets. I had never seen anything like it. The sidewalks were jammed with people, the stores were filled with customers, lights were blazing, and there was an amazing air of business and prosperity. In size, the town did not differ greatly from Utica, but the part of it in which I now found myself was radically different from the part of Utica where my store was located. Right away, I felt that Lancaster was the place for me.

"After spending a couple of hours walking around the business part of the city, and getting my supper in a cheap restaurant, I found a hotel—a vile old one it was, too—where I got lodgings for fifty cents. Early next morning I started out to find a vacant store, and at Number 170 North Queen street I found one that promised to meet my requirements. After concluding arrangements for the place, I took the first train for

Utica, arriving there almost stranded financially, but with my hopes renewed and my purpose strong."

There was still the problem of getting out of Utica with clean heels, and of obtaining sufficient cash or credit to stock the new store. Fortunately, there was enough cash in the bank to pay the Utica bills; and Moore & Smith, in response to a glowing letter from Woolworth, offered him additional credit up to $300. For William H. Moore it was bread cast upon the waters, as the sequel will show.

Woolworth locked his door in Utica on June 11, and opened his modest Lancaster location exactly ten days later. The date, June 21, 1879, marks the launching of the first successful (and what is now the oldest) five-and-ten-cent store in the world. Also, it was the first store to deal exclusively in five-*and-ten*-cent merchandise. Although Woolworth retained for a time the Great Five Cent Store sign, other signs over the 14-foot Lancaster front read: "5 and 10 Cent Store" and "Woolworth's 5 and 10 cent store."

On opening day, the Lancaster store carried $410 worth of stock—the leftover Utica goods plus Moore & Smith's new shipment. Thirty per cent of the stock was sold the first day, and Woolworth felt he had a winner. At once he began to plan expansion. The next day he wrote a joyful card to his father which has been preserved and is now in the possession of his brother, Charles S. Woolworth. It reads:

Lancaster, Pa., June 22nd, 1879.

Dear Father: I opened my store here for trade yesterday and did not advertise any. No one knew there was a 5¢ store in this city until Friday night and we managed to sell yesterday in one day $127.65 which is the most I ever sold in one day.

We sold $80 in the evening alone. I had 7 clerks
and they had to work you bet. We could have sold
$200 if the store had been larger. Jennie helped
me last night. . . . I think some of starting a branch
store in Harrisburg, Pa. and putting Sum in it if
Moore & Smith will spare him. Direct—

> F. W. Woolworth
> 170 North Queen St.,
> Lancaster, Pa.

The Lancaster store continued to prove highly
popular with the Pennsylvania Dutch housewives, and
Proprietor Woolworth fondled his expansion ideas. He
kept his overhead expenses to a minimum, watching
his clerks like a hawk for breakage and theft, working
them long hours and at low wages. He figured expenses to the penny. Invariably on Saturday nights
and even some mid-week evenings Jennie came in to
lend a hand. Often, on these occasions, year-old baby
Lena was placed out of sight under the counter in an
improvised crib, made out of a packing box, and
gurgled away happily as the bargain-hungry customers
shuffled past. Packages were wrapped in old newspapers which he bought at two cents a pound from
a local newspaper and lugged to the store on his
shoulders. Standard wrapping paper still cost eight
cents a pound.

"Mr. Woolworth sat on the platform of a winding
stairway at the back of the store, guarding the sales
box and watching the clerks at work," says Mrs. Susan
Kane of Lancaster, only surviving member of Woolworth's original sales force. "There were three of us
and we were paid $1.50 a week. We were not assigned
to any particular one of the counters, which lined the
large center aisle, but just followed the customers
around. After we made a sale we walked back to Mr.

Woolworth to get change. He entered each sale on a tablet and added up at night. Our best sellers were tinware, toys, washbasins, wash towels, handkerchiefs and ribbons."

The result of the proprietor's economies and careful management soon showed in a fattening bank balance; and early in July Woolworth wrote his brother in Watertown that he had taken a store in Harrisburg, thirty-five miles from Lancaster, and offered Sumner seven dollars a week to manage it.

C. S. (Sumner) Woolworth was developing into an able salesman under the watchful eye of W. H. Moore. Earlier in the year he had been sent to open a five-cent store in Copenhagen, a small town some fourteen miles from Watertown. He was thorough and reliable, as well as fun-loving.

When Sumner arrived in Harrisburg, he found himself master of a mere hole-in-the-wall, 12 feet wide by 16 deep. The rent was $5 a week and the salary list, including Brother Sumner's $7, exactly $11 a week.

The Harrisburg store was a repetition of the Utica experiment. Opening July 19, the tiny emporium enjoyed a first day's sale of $85.41; and for several weeks kept up a good pace. Then came a steady decline, broken only by a sales revival during Christmas week. Finally, in March, 1880, Woolworth decided to give it up and seek a new pasture. It is surprising in retrospect to note that this man, who had never traveled, had the ability so early in his career always to try a new town, to expand, to think in as big a territorial way as he did.

For his new location, Woolworth settled upon York, Pennsylvania, and opened there April 3, 1880. The Lancaster store was doing so well that Sumner's salary, as manager at York, was boosted to eight dollars a week.

The York store, too, was tiny with pocket-size show

windows, and, like Utica and Harrisburg it started out
with a flourish. Sales for the first twelve weeks, as
listed in the Woolworth records, were:

First week	$222.52
Second week	176.46
Third week	90.80
Fourth week	107.94
Fifth week	76.97
Sixth week	62.99
Seventh week	41.95
Eighth week	45.20
Ninth week	46.54
Tenth week	46.25
Eleventh week	38.70
Twelfth week	35.60

When sales evaporated to a rock-bottom low of
$3.05 on June 25, Woolworth decided to add York to
his other defeats.

"In my three months in York, we sold about $1,000
worth of goods," recalls C. S. Woolworth. "Our net
profit was exactly $36. We shut up shop in York the
last day in June, shipped what stock we had there to
Lancaster and I went to work in the Lancaster store.
But we had no thought of resting on our oars. In our
spare time that summer we traveled all over the surrounding territory, looking for another good location,
and finally decided to make our next bid in Scranton,
Pa. The Scranton store became the second oldest five-
and-ten-cent in the world and Scranton was a good
choice for me. I've been here ever since."

The Scranton site was a spacious room at 125 Penn
Avenue. The rent was $35 a month. The opening date
was November 6, 1880. Says C. S. Woolworth:

"The space was so large that we had to build a partition about two-thirds of the way back in order to make a decent showing of our stock—and we had to spread it out pretty thin in spots at that!"

The Scranton venture opened under the sign "Woolworth Bros. 5 & 10 Cent Store" but on the sidewalk, partly festooned with tin pans, was Frank Woolworth's proud old Utica sign: "The Great 5 Cent Store." At "Sum" Woolworth's boarding house fellow lodgers greeted him jovially as The Great Five.

The old account book of C. S. Woolworth shows that sales on opening day, a Saturday, were $43.20; and for the first week $242.08. The second week dipped to $137.11, but Christmas week boomed sales to $621.71, with $235.07 taken in on Christmas Eve. In January there was a reaction, with the top week showing only $72.01; and sales on one stormy day actually dropped to but $5.95.

"Soon, however, the business got its balance," recollects C. S. Woolworth, "and the first year we did a trade of a little more than $9,000. That was enough to make us a tidy net profit and let the other storekeepers know there was another fish in their pond. Incidentally, the prejudice against us among other merchants was very strong. In order to exist we had to offer what bargains we could and undersell other stores on certain items. Naturally this didn't tend to make for that spirit of brotherly comradeship which should obtain among fellow practitioners of commerce. In fact"—he chuckled—"one of our rivals christened us The Corsicans after a melodrama about some bandits that was popular in the opera houses of those days."

So long as he was making money Frank Woolworth took such criticism in smiling part.

Woolworth's chief problem now was merchandise— to find new novelties which could be sold for five and

ten cents. Jobbers found the tall, blue-eyed young
man a hard, shrewd bargainer who knew the market
thoroughly and would not invest a penny unless he
could foresee sales returns. In the fragment of autobiography to which we have referred, Woolworth tells
how he first discovered Christmas tree ornaments:

In the fall of 1880 I went to an importing firm
on Strawberry Street, Philadelphia, Meyer &
Schoenaman, to buy some toys and about the
first thing they did was to drag out a lot of
colored glass ornaments the like of which I had
never before seen.

"What are those things?" I asked.

They explained that these goods were, oh,
such fine sellers, but I laughed.

"You can't sell me any foolish things like that,"
I said. "I don't believe they would sell and most
of them would be smashed anyway before there
was a chance to sell them."

They explained that the profit was big enough
to offset the breakage, but I was incredulous.
It was hard to understand what the people would
want of those colored glass things.

We argued back and forth a long time and
finally the house made me the proposition that
it would guarantee the sale, at retail, of twenty-
five dollars worth of the Christmas tree ornaments.

"All right," I agreed. "You can send them to me
wholly at your own risk."

The goods arrived a few days before Christmas and, with a great deal of indifference, I put
them on my counters. In two days they were all
gone, and I woke up. But it was too late to order
any more, and I had to turn away a big demand.
The next Christmas season I was on hand early

with what I considered a large order, but it was not large enough. They proved to be the best sellers in my store for the holidays.

Variety was what he must offer his customers. Any new item was important. Some that he discovered, some that were thrust upon him (such as the Christmas ornaments) grossed millions in the years that followed.

In Lancaster, the Woolworths lived simply in a two-story brick house on Lemon street. Mrs. Woolworth's sister, Sidney Creighton, had come down from Canada to help with the housework. Mrs. Susan Kane recalls: "On Sunday afternoons we clerks would be invited there—often. The atmosphere was very pleasant."

Frank Woolworth paid his debts and started a savings account.

"By the end of 1880 I was so rich that I decided to take the first vacation I had ever enjoyed," he reminisced years later when his stores numbered hundreds. "I was worth $2,000, which looked bigger to me then than $20,000,000 would now. In fact, I felt quite as rich then as I do now because I had the consciousness and the satisfaction of having made a success in business."

The vacation took the Woolworths back to Watertown—and what a triumphant homecoming it was. Jennie in a new dress generously draped in the back and trimmed with fringe, an infinitesimal hat with feathers perched high on her head, smiled happily beneath her parasol as she promenaded the public square, her arm firmly entrenched in Frank's; while not even a copious mustache could conceal the latter's exuberance as he lifted his new bowler hat and shouted greetings to old acquaintances.

The proudest moment of all was when they entered
the store of Moore & Smith. Moore left his platform
desk to greet them; Mrs. Coons left a customer to
come and kiss them both, not even dreaming that
some day she would be the manager of a store in the
Woolworth Syndicate. Fred Kirby joined the cluster.
An errand boy when Woolworth went away two
years before, he was now bookkeeper and had charge
of what was left of Moore & Smith's five-and-ten
jobbing department.

Kirby was only one of dozens of Watertown young
men who were tempted to seek a fortune in five and
ten just from listening. Frank Woolworth's exuberance was contagious. Moreover, Woolworth was
ready to go partners with Kirby in a store, if he could
get a little capital. But Kirby's parents vetoed the
plan; he was too young. How they would have
gasped if made aware they were holding him back
from something that was going to make it possible
for him in years ahead philanthropically to bestow
$60,000,000!

Elsewhere on the square Woolworth gave out
enthusiasm for his chosen field. Ceaselessly for several
generations young men had been detaching themselves from this community; had gone away to hard-
ships in California, Colorado and the Dakotas. A few
had made money, some had taken to drink or had
been scalped by Indians, so it was reported. But who
could name anyone to compare with Frank Woolworth? He had returned successful in less than two
years! At Bushnell's store Woolworth found his friend
Harry Moody, twenty years old now and talking
about a department store job in Rochester. Frank
promised to keep him in mind—and did.

Young Carson Peck was with Moody and Woolworth as they talked. When Woolworth had fallen ill,

Peck "temporarily" had taken his place in the Bushnell store; he was still there and restless. Peck was a member of a distinguished old family in Woolworth's home county. The young man had attended St. Lawrence University for a year, taught school a while and had counted himself lucky to get Frank's job. Subsequently Carson Peck started with Woolworth as half owner and manager of a store in Utica.

Another drygoods clerk there on the public square who grew into a millionaire through his later association with Woolworth was Clinton Pierce Case. He, too, was a native of Jefferson County. He was clerking for Campbell & Moulton, general drygoods merchants, when Woolworth came home. He was restless in his employment from the day Woolworth said his farewells and returned to Lancaster. However, that was not until the visitors had excited numerous relations.

Naturally they visited prosperous Uncle Albon McBrier. His son, Edwin, Frank's first cousin, during this visit heard at first hand the exciting advantages about five and ten which afterward lured him into the business as partner in a store, eventually to become one of the millionaires of five and ten. Another McBrier, Aunt Jane, was wife to James Knox, a farmer. She let it be known she was going to write to her son, Seymour Knox. Seymour was at this time twenty, about two years younger than Sumner Woolworth. A smart lad, his mother boasted. At fifteen he had been teacher in a country school. At seventeen he had started west and found employment as a store clerk in Hart, Michigan. Frank would hear from him, Aunt Jane promised. Among the Woolworths scattered around the county were Fred and Herbert, third cousins to Frank. They were just children then, but it seemed no time at all before careers had been marked out for them in five and ten. Herbert (who clerked for a while in a Watertown hat store) was the stubborn one who later tried to create a chain of his own, ending with nothing.

The early Woolworth records show that sales for 1881 reached $18,000; and for 1882 jumped to $24,125. Though three of his first five ventures had failed, Woolworth was now proprietor of one flourishing and one moderately successful store. He seemed justified in looking upon himself as a man of some substance.

And his ambition for further expansion in his chosen field was stronger than ever.

Chapter V

Early Expansion

AS HE sat on the platform in the rear of his Lancaster store, making change for his three salesgirls and surveying his small world, Woolworth's head was full of dreams and schemes. The thought uppermost in his mind was expansion. If one small shop such as the Scranton store could earn him a profit of $1,000 or more each year, why couldn't he do even better with other and larger stores?

It was obvious to him that the five-and-ten-cent business, based as it was upon large and quick turnovers, needed numerous outlets. A chain of stores would enable him to purchase goods on a scale big enough to attract new kinds of merchandise. As yet, this market was extremely limited. Also, the more goods he bought the cheaper he could sell them.

One lesson Woolworth had learned and learned well: never again would he go into debt, never again would he go through the torture of notes or creditors' judgments hanging over his head.

Since more capital was essential and he refused to borrow, he began searching for partners with a little cash, men who would share half the risks in opening each new store in return for half its profits. He found partner number one right in the family—his Aunt Jane McBrier Knox's bright boy, Seymour.

Seymour Horace Knox, after seven years of clerking in a Michigan store, had some money saved. He was twenty-four years old in 1884 when he came down to Lancaster for a talk with Cousin Frank, who was thirty-two.

On September 20, 1884, the firm of Woolworth & Knox opened a store in Reading, Pa. It did well, but after a year Knox was disposed to try a bigger field and as Woolworth was ready to venture with him, Knox's half interest was sold to a resident of Reading, A. H. Satterthwait, who became manager of the store.

Woolworth produced money to meet Knox's capital and they opened a store in Newark, N. J. This city baffled them. One day Woolworth interrupted a buying trip to visit his partner-cousin and found him downcast. Business was terrible. Knox showed Woolworth a letter from his mother. She had written she was helping him all she could by sending him "quite a lot" of money she had saved. The amount was $40.

"Hold on a while," urged Woolworth. "Keep your expenses down as much as you can, and I'll look around for a new location."

Eventually they kept a rendezvous in Erie, Pa. Knox had closed the Newark store and shipped the stock to Erie. The store had a frontage of 22 feet, a depth of 150 feet. On their counters they had arranged a stock sixfold greater than Woolworth had displayed when he opened in Lancaster. Its value was $2,492.75. No wonder they passed a sleepless night in a hotel room which they shared to save expenses. They dressed early to direct the opening. It was an anticlimax. By actual count twenty-five customers came into the store that morning. The streets were crowded, but even when the noon whistles were blowing the store remained practically empty. They left a clerk in charge and tried vainly to cheer themselves with a restaurant dinner. Afterward they walked in the city park, dreading a return to a store with empty aisles. But finally they started back. As they came around a corner and saw the freshly painted red front, they felt as if a miracle had saved them. The store was jammed to the doors!

While they had dawdled in the restaurant and strolled in the park, farmers' wagons had been rolling into town for shopping expeditions. This new store was a treat for the women and the children. Men of the town, of course, were penned at their jobs until six o'clock, Saturdays no exception. But Saturday, last thing, a man collected his pay and Saturday night all over America was when folks did their shopping. When the cousins counted up the sales cash that night they had $213.25. The opening was a true omen of success; this store became a steady money maker.

Meanwhile, Woolworth had been experiencing individual downs and ups. The downs included a short-lived incursion into the 25-cent store field in Reading and Lancaster; and a try at establishing a five-and-ten in Philadelphia which ended in three months with a loss of $380. The ups included a successful reinvasion of Harrisburg, Pa., and a new store in Trenton, N. J. His partner in Harrisburg was a local man, H. H. Hesslet, and in Trenton, Oscar Woodworth.

It was Woolworth's brother, Sumner, who brought Oscar Woodworth, a New Yorker of some means, into the fold. On a train bound for New York he and Woodworth, a fellow passenger, struck up a chance conversation which resulted in Woodworth inviting him to stay at his home over night. Sumner told his new friend about his brother Frank's commercial adventures and eventually brought the two together. The result was that Woodworth became Frank Woolworth's partner in the Trenton store. The relationship proved pleasant and profitable for both.

By now, Sumner Woolworth was firmly rooted in Scranton. The store was a success—so much so that Sumner purchased Frank's half-interest out of his profits and became sole proprietor. Their business parting was entirely amicable. It was merely a matter of Sumner wishing to remain where he was and to own his own business.

Also, the younger brother was struggling to make a go of a small five-and-ten which he had opened in near-by Wilkes-Barre, in partnership with his former Watertown store chum, Fred M. Kirby.

Fred Kirby, tall, solemn, of Scotch descent, had now turned twenty-one, and won the consent of his parents to his entry into five-and-ten. He had managed to save and borrow $600 for the Wilkes-Barre venture with Sumner Woolworth.

Meanwhile, Frank Woolworth continued to expand.

He opened a store in Elmira, New York, with Earl Northrup and another in Easton, Pennsylvania, with A. Getman, whose son managed the business.

The partnership principle, Woolworth found, had been a happy choice. Not only did the partners supply capital, but their active management was far more efficient than that of salaried managers.

By the fall of 1886, either with Knox or other partners, Woolworth controlled seven stores. The list, together with the date opened, the size of the store, the amount of stock on opening day, and the first day's sales, is:

Lancaster, Pa., opened June 21, 1879; size of store,

35 feet by 14; amount of stock opening day, $410; first day's sales, $127.65. Reading, Pa., Sept. 20, 1884; 45 by 16; $1,531; $209.20. Harrisburg, Pa., August 8, 1885; 40 by 15; $1,615; $196.73. Trenton, N. J., Sept. 5, 1885; 90 by 15; $2,192; $353.55. Erie, Pa., August 28, 1886; 150 by 22; $2,492.75; $213.25. Elmira, N. Y., Oct. 16, 1886; 45 by 15; $2,245.35; $29.05. Easton, Pa., Oct. 23, 1886; 46 by 16; $2,299.55; $170.40.

Although several other sites, in addition to those we have mentioned, had been tried and abandoned, it may be noted from the dates that Woolworth hadn't moved with precipitate haste. He felt, with as fair certainty as one could in so new a field, that he could now select successful locations. Capable men to run the stores and the ever-present problem of merchandise were his chief concerns. For his partners and managers he wanted sober, industrious young men who would work the clock around and obey instructions. Wherever possible, he wanted the family type of man, for in many of his stores the manager was the only male employee. By displaying goods on counters, where the customer could make his own selection, Woolworth had eliminated the need of salesmanship in his stores. All that his clerks had to do was wrap packages and make change. This distinctly Woolworth innovation in American business enabled him to employ young girls at wages far lower than that of the average clerk—an important item in a business where profits were based on pennies.

In 1885, while on a visit to his father, who was still living on the Great Bend farm with a second wife, Elvira Austin Moulton, his former housekeeper, Woolworth learned that his old firm, Moore & Smith, was about to go into bankruptcy. Perry R. Smith, the junior partner, had withdrawn and gone West. William H. Moore was the sole proprietor.

Woolworth promptly offered to stock the man who had first stocked him. Moore gratefully accepted and the famous Watertown Corner Store—where the five-and-ten idea was incubated in the East—became itself a five-and-ten. It remains so today, with a plaque in the window commemorating it as the birthplace of the five-and-ten.

By 1886 Woolworth found himself in command of a snug little business doing a trade of almost $100,000 a year and earning a net profit of some $10,000. Though profits depended upon a variety of elements, *the main one was* intelligent buying. Woolworth himself personally bought every article that went on the shelves of his seven stores, and as business expanded this required more and more of his time. Novelty manufacturers and jobbers were scattered all along the Atlantic seaboard but New York City was their main market.

So to New York Woolworth moved in July, 1886, to lay the foundation of what was to become the world's largest retail buying organization.

That was the year the Statue of Liberty was unveiled in New York Harbor and Steve Brodie did (or did not) jump off the new Brooklyn Bridge. New York—which then meant only Manhattan—was a city of low buildings, cobbled paving and horse cars. The population of some 1,250,000 was pushing rapidly north on both sides of Central Park. Squatters, ousted only a few years before from the Grand Central area, still clung, with their dogs and goats, to their nondescript shanties on rocky vacant land further uptown. The steam-driven East and West Side elevated railways dropped ashes and sometimes live cinders on pedestrians and horses alike. Many downtown residences had been remodeled for business purposes. Goods were swung to the top floors by means of rope hoists and a common sign was: "Danger! Look out for the hoist!"

Woolworth took $25-a-month desk room at 105 Chambers Street, and rented a small house at 365A Quincy street, Brooklyn, for his family. Two more children born in Lancaster, Edna and Jessie May, now swelled the family to five. The eldest child Helena, or Lena as she was called, was eight years old; Edna, who was to become the mother of Barbara Hutton, was approaching her third birthday, and the baby, Jessie, was three months old when the family moved to Brooklyn. All three children were buxom, round-faced and resembled their mother. The family kept no servant, but Mrs. Woolworth's sister, Sidney Creighton, still lived with them and assisted in the household duties.

The novelty jobbers and manufacturers clustered along lower Broadway and adjacent side streets were a hard, sharp lot. But those who hadn't met Woolworth before, soon realized that they were dealing with one of the shrewdest buyers that had ever come to New York. The bold, handsome young newcomer soon won their grudging respect. He *knew* merchandise.

In his quest for a greater variety of low-cost goods, Woolworth soon learned that prices were kept high by the jobbers, who had the inside track with the manufacturers. Time and again he tried to crash through the ring of middlemen to deal directly with the manufacturers—only to be bluntly reminded that he was merely a retailer and, as such, custom and policy decreed that he must buy through jobbers. This would have thwarted a less persistent individual, but Woolworth believed if he could prove by a concrete example that a manufacturer could make more money by selling to him directly it would serve as a wedge to other manufacturers. Candy turned out to be his concrete example.

For a long time he had had the idea of selling candy at five cents, in quarter-pound lots. The whole-sale price of good candy then ranged from twenty-five cents to a dollar a pound. Woolworth journeyed all over New York and talked with a dozen large manufacturers. None was interested. In fact, they called the scheme harebrained and told him flatly that good candy could not even be made for twenty cents a pound.

"But we intend to sell large quantities," argued Woolworth, "and that ought to bring your costs down."

"How do you know you can sell large amounts?" one manufacturer asked, hinting that he might be interested in an order for, say, ten thousand pounds.

When Woolworth had to confess that the whole scheme was experimental and that he wouldn't dare risk an order for more than a few hundred pounds, the candy nabob stonily dismissed him.

The repeated rebuffs only spurred Woolworth's determination. Then one day, walking on Wooster Street, west of Broadway, he spied a sign over a small candy shop: "D. Arnould." He went in, introduced himself to Mr. Arnould, who turned out to be a pleasant, approachable gentleman, and explained his difficulty. Arnould did not seem to think the idea particularly revolutionary.

"You say you have to sell candy at five cents the quarter pound?" he asked.

"Yes, or we cannot sell it at all," replied Wool-worth.

"Well, come back and see me tomorrow. I'll think it over and see what I can do."

The next day Arnould smilingly showed Woolworth a list of several varieties which could be made to sell for twenty cents a pound, with a small margin of profit. Woolworth was so jubilant that he immediately ordered one hundred pounds of candy for each of the stores—mixed chocolates, chocolate creams, marshmallows, hard candies.

Then he hurried out to purchase scales and glass trays—and to break the news by letter to the store managers. The latter were aghast and protested as one man. Candy was perishable and hard to handle. The public wouldn't buy it in a five-and-ten store, and so on.

Woolworth's answer was a letter giving detailed instructions on how to weigh, display and sell the candy, and designating a certain Saturday morning as the date of an opening sale. By nightfall on that Saturday, every last piece of candy was gone and the stores were clamoring for more. The public liked having its sweet tooth tickled for a nickel.

That was the beginning of one of the most popular lines ever tried in the five-and-tens. Arnould's little shop became a great factory and store on Canal Street. Over the years other candy manufacturers fell into line. Today one-seventh of the candy consumed in the United States is purchased in the five-and-tens. Woolworth stores sell some 250,000,000 pounds of candy a year, at a profit of approximately $3,000,000.

Once, in Philadelphia, Woolworth searched out a little factory, just store width, where a man was turning by hand a small machine which transformed gold tinsel into garlands. There were two or three girls at work making other Christmas tree ornaments. The boss, Bernard Wilmsen, spoke little English. But he made it plain that everything he had made or was making would go to jobbers.

"My jobbers can't supply me," pleaded Woolworth.

In broken English, Wilmsen repeated that the stock lining shelves in a small room at the rear was sold. But Woolworth was a jolly visitor who appeared not to understand "no." He coaxed and made himself agreeable until at last the young immigrant manufacturer said: "All right. I give you what I have. For the others I'll make some more."

"There!" declared Woolworth. "Now I'm going to keep on buying from you for life!"

In 1939, when Mr. Wilmsen was eighty-one, he said: "Mr. Woolworth had at that time only a few stores. But I grew with Woolworth. I have sold them at least $25,000,000 worth of Christmas tree ornaments, in one year $800,000 worth. At first we imported tinsel from Germany. Since the war I make it myself. Today, at the corner of Haegert and Jasper streets I have a big factory. I have 225 people working to fill Woolworth orders. We sell to all, but Woolworth was first. I am the oldest Woolworth supplier."

On one of his frequent trips exploring for possible store locations, Woolworth landed one day in 1887 in Akron, Ohio, and called upon his old boss, Perry Smith, of Moore & Smith, who was now operating a five-and-ten there. Surveying Smith's counters, he spied some white china cups, saucers and plates. Smith told him where they could be purchased, and soon, in the Woolworth stores, the new ware was pushing tin plates and cups into the background. The profits were small but they attracted a new and better class of customers.

At the end of his first year in New York, the result of Woolworth's candy merchandising showed sufficient sales and profit that he felt justified in leasing an office of his own. He took a room in a loft at 321 Broadway, with the front part railed off and used as an office. In the rear he stored a small stock of merchandise, which was shipped to the stores as wanted. This loft room was dingy, yet over the door was a gleaming sign:

Office of
F. W. WOOLWORTH
Buyer and Manager
for the
WOOLWORTH SYNDICATE
Strictly 5 and 10
cent stores

That fall of 1887, Woolworth and Knox enlisted another recruit, their young first cousin, Edwin Merton McBrier, Uncle Albon McBrier's son, and with him opened a store in Lockport, New York. Edwin McBrier put up $1,000 for a half-interest in this establishment and agreed to manage it. Woolworth and Knox each took a quarter-interest.

The following year Woolworth hired as office assistant a young bookkeeper named Alvin Edgar Ivie. Although but sixteen, Ivie had already put in two years of all-round business apprenticeship in the office of the Manhattan Brass Company, at Twenty-eighth Street and First Avenue, where his father was a superintendent. He was strong, blue-eyed and ambitious. Today he is a wealthy retired Woolworth veteran, with a city mansion and a country place in New Hampshire.

"Through a church librarian," says Mr. Ivie, "I heard that a Mr. Woolworth was looking for an office helper and I went down and applied for the job. Woolworth, one could tell right away, was the kind of man who knew exactly what he wanted. After a few questions and a quick size-up, he offered me $8 a week and I grabbed the job. Woolworth was a big man, just under six feet. He wore a mustache and his forehead was high and broad. By contrast, the lower part of his face, from the nose down, seemed thin. Later when his weight went up, that part of his face filled in.

"I had been used to hard work but I'd never seen a worker like Mr. Woolworth. He seemed able to keep going all the time. He made decisions quickly, then stuck by them. But he was always ready to take time out for a joke and if you did your work he took you right to his heart.

"On September 1, 1888, the office was moved from 321 Broadway to the old Stewart Building, 280 Broadway, at the northeast corner of Broadway and Chambers Street, where for a month we occupied Room 242 on the fifth floor. This was found to be too small and on October 1 the office was changed to a larger room, 238, on the Reade Street side of the building, which remained headquarters for several years. I was Woolworth's only employee in this office until the latter part of November, 1888, when a young woman typist, Miss Tallman, was engaged. Before that Woolworth handled every detail of the business himself, attending to all orders, writing all letters in long hand."

Woolworth kept in close daily touch with the stores and watched over them like a mother hen, sending voluminous memoranda and instructions on tissue sheets, manifolded upon an old-fashioned letter press machine. For instance:

To push trade in dull season, keep your goods in attractive shape as possible and trim your windows twice a week with big leaders with prices attached on each article and if necessary

sell a few leaders for 10 cents. Among good
leaders I can mention such things as two quart
glass pitchers that cost $1 per dozen and about
2 dozen in a barrel. They will cost you about
$1.35 to lay down in your store. A lamp with
burner and chimney to sell complete is also a
good leader and costs about $1.15 laid down. . . .
Another thing you must watch close in dull
season is your expense account. Be sure and not
have more clerks than you can possibly use and
don't turn all the gas burners on every night.
The same applies to coal. Watch your freight
bills. Some of you have got the habit of placing
goods that cost $5, $5.50 or $6 per gross on the
5-cent counter without looking at the article to
see if you can get 10 cents for it or not. Because
the goods were bought cheap is no reason they
should always be sold cheap. Put leaders to the
front. That is our mode of advertising.

In 1888 the Woolworth Syndicate opened five new
stores: in Utica, N. Y.; Poughkeepsie, N. Y.; Wilmington, Delaware; Allentown, Pa.; and Buffalo, N. Y.
These were in charge, respectively, of Carson C.
Peck, Mary A. Creighton, Baron W. Gage, Clinton P.
Case and Seymour H. Knox. Peck, Gage and, of
course, Knox were partners; Miss Creighton and Case
managers. Mary Ann Creighton, a favorite sister-in-
law of Woolworth, had the distinction of becoming
the first and one of the few women store managers.
Clinton Pierce Case was the Jefferson County man
who had clerked for Campbell & Moulton in Watertown. He was destined for high place in the Woolworth organization.

Meanwhile the energetic young sparkplug of the
syndicate traveled constantly, taking upon his own

shoulders all the details of the openings, the display of merchandise, and so on, in addition to his duties in the New York office.

The strain became too great. His weight dropped to 135 pounds. His large frame again became gaunt and bony. One evening in early December, while working late in his uncarpeted, cheerless office, he complained to his young bookkeeper Ivie of a pain in the back. The next morning he did not appear at 8.30 A.M. as usual. Instead, later in the day came a post card—there were, of course, no telephones then—from Mrs. Woolworth to Ivie:

"Mr. Woolworth has been taken down sick and asks you to come here and bring the mail."

Ivie tied the mail into a package and boarded a cable car over the new Brooklyn Bridge. Transferring to the Fulton Street "L" line, he reached his employer's Quincy Street home in the late afternoon. The house was hushed, and even the two younger Woolworth daughters seemed to sense that something was wrong. Mrs. Woolworth told Ivie the doctor had diagnosed her husband's illness as typhoid fever and had ordered complete rest.

Woolworth lay desperately ill for weeks but refused to lose touch with his business.

"For two months," recalls Ivie, "I took the mail and the orders to his house each day. On all but two of these occasions, when he was delirious, he gave me directions and instructions as to how to carry on the business. It was quite a responsibility for a boy but in those two months I learned a lot about the business and a lot about the boss. I certainly admired his courage and grit. He was confined to his home all during December, 1888, and January, 1889."

Weak and shaken, Woolworth returned to active

duty early in February. Years later he said this illness really marked the beginning of his success, explaining that it broke him of the conceit that only he himself could handle every detail of the business.

"From then on," observed Woolworth, "I made up my mind to place responsibilities on other people, to confine myself to general supervision—looking ahead, thinking up new plans, developing a broader outlook. So many merchants never get over the conceit that they must do everything themselves, with the result that they straggle along in one little store. A business is like a snowball: one man can easily push it along for a while but the snowball becomes so large if pushed ahead that help must be obtained to roll it—and if you don't keep rolling it, it will soon melt. No business can stand stationary for any considerable period. It either rises or falls and, if left to itself, the tendency is for it to fall."

To help push his five-and-ten snowball ahead, Woolworth chose one of his partner-managers to share the executive burdens. He was Carson C. Peck of the Utica store, whom we have met before.

Born January 10, 1858, at Stone Mills, New York, Peck, whose parents died when he was young, was reared by his uncle, Capt. Abner Peck, sheriff of Jefferson County.

During Woolworth's expanding years, the two men kept in touch, and Woolworth was delighted when Peck offered to become a five-and-ten partner, and to manage a store. Peck borrowed the capital and took charge of a new store at 153 Genesee Street, Utica, opened July 21, 1888. The store did splendidly from the start. Peck's success in Utica, where Woolworth had failed, did not lower the latter's respect for him.

With his keen, talent-seeking eyes Woolworth had watched Peck's progress. Then one day, late in 1889, he dropped off a train in Utica and invited Peck for a walk. As they strolled along Genesee Street, Woolworth said:

"Peck, I came here to offer you the opportunity of a lifetime. I need a manager and buyer in the New York office. If you will take the job, I'll see that you make more money than you're making now and you will make a great deal more in the future. What do you say?"

After a consultation with his wife, Peck said yes, and it was arranged that he should come to New York at the beginning of the new year. He became Woolworth's general manager and was his right-hand man for a quarter of a century. At the same time Woolworth bought out Peck's interest in the Utica store.

This was not the only change within the syndicate. With five years of practical experience behind him, Seymour Knox decided that he wanted to branch out for himself. Accordingly, Woolworth sold Knox his interest in the Erie, Lockport, and Buffalo stores and used the capital to open stores in Syracuse, New York, and New Haven, Connecticut. As manager in Syracuse he installed Mrs. A. E. Coons, the matronly, middle-aged woman of engaging personality, who had been chief saleslady at Moore & Smith's; and for the New Haven post he selected one of his wife's brothers, Allen Creighton.

Excluding the Buffalo, Lockport and Erie stores, sales for 1889 totaled $247,214.26, and Woolworth jubilantly wrote his managers and manager-partners that "this is a big pile of five-and-ten-cent goods to sell in a year." In the same "General Letter," as he called his communications, he chided the managers for carelessness in making out orders:

New York, January 4, 1890.

You must now prepare yourselves for a good talking to. I have been obliged to get a new Typewriter and she is not as much accustomed to your writing as I am and Miss Tallman the Lady I had before and I wish you would make a special effort when you make out orders to have them only one item on a line, only one firm on a page, and write on only one side of the sheet and use the cost marks to designate the cost of the goods and above all things write them plain so a person can read them and each word in full without abbreviations. After you have made out your orders give them to one of your girls to look over and see if they can read and understand them and that will be proof enough. . . . I expect Mr. Peck here tomorrow and he will be ready to commence work in New York office next week. The clerks in Trenton and Syracuse stores have the "Grippe" and they all seem to be afflicted more or less. Only two stores have sent in inventory yet. Remember all bills bearing date of December, 1889, go under last year's report and should be added to your inventory no matter if the goods did not arrive until after January 1.

In more jocular vein, Woolworth told of a visit of his women managers to New York:

"The Lady Members of the WOOLWORTH SYNDICATE, Mrs. Coons and Miss Mate

(Mary) Creighton are in New York having a
grand time. They have not been in the lockup
yet but they were locked out at my house last
Saturday midnight and finally got us woke up
after they had aroused all the neighbors."

The Woolworth home now was a substantial
brownstone house at 209 Jefferson Avenue, Brooklyn,
which he had purchased. Here he frequently entertained his business associates, and brought them together, at least once a year, for what he termed a
Grand Five and Ten Reunion. These reunions lasted
two or three days and were jolly affairs, generally
culminating in a picnic or a seashore excursion, with
plenty of food and liquid refreshment.

With his personal profits running to more than
$1,000 a month, the hustling head of the Woolworth
Syndicate began to feel himself a man of substance.
One warm summer day—the date was July 31, 1889
—he sat at his desk and dashed off a single-sheet will
in longhand, leaving everything of which he might
die possessed, unconditionally, to his wife. He tucked
it among other papers and didn't think about another
will for almost thirty years.

Woolworth had a reason for putting his affairs in
order. He was planning his first trip to Europe. He
had made friends with B. F. Hunt, Jr., buyer and
acting partner of Horace Partridge & Company,
largest importers of toys in the United States; and
Hunt had suggested that Woolworth accompany him
to Europe the following winter.

"You can buy toys over there a whole lot cheaper,"
explained Hunt, "and the trip will broaden you and
your vision of markets."

So, having coached Carson Peck in his new duties,
Woolworth sailed off to Europe on the *City of Paris*

February 19, 1890, with Mr. Hunt. His letters, excerpts from which appear in the chapter following, furnish not only the story of his toy-buying expedition but a most revealing portrait of Woolworth himself at that stage of his career.

Chapter VI
_____

European Interlude

KEEN, observant, if sometimes naive, Woolworth's frequent and voluminous letters describing his first European trip are as fresh and interesting as though penned yesterday. Written in longhand, on trains, boats, by candlelight, these so-called "General Letters" were mailed to New York, multigraphed and distributed to Woolworth's business associates.

There was a final admonition to the boys before departure of himself and his friend Hunt:

New York, February 15, 1890.
This is my last General Letter to your before sailing. Remember my address in Europe will be as follows: F. W. Woolworth, care of Eggers & Stallforth, Bremen, Germany. And postage on letters to Bremen is five cents per half ounce so you must use thin paper and envelopes to save expense. . . . I have everything ready to go including a rubber mackintosh, two pairs of Arctic overshoes, heavy underwear, lap robe, steamer trunk, steamer cap, traveling valise, soap, medicine etc. And a Number 2 Kodak Camera. I notice some of the bank accounts are

getting low. Now you must be very careful and not order more goods than you can pay for while I am away.

The next communication was a quick note from shipboard:

> February 19 on board steamer "City of Paris"
> The agony is over and my Dear Friends that came to see me off have just gone home; and we are left to the mercy of the elements. I must confess that when it came to the final farewell a frog came up in my throat and I could say nothing but I have been trying hard since to get it out; and will be all right in the morning. Frog up in my throat again; so I shall stop writing and mail this and go to bed. Good bye.
> Yours truly,
> F. W. Woolworth.

The *City of Paris* was the Inman Line's luxurious twin-screw steamship which held the trans-Atlantic record, Liverpool to New York, of 5 days, 19 hours, 18 minutes. Before the current voyage was over, Woolworth was wishing the crack liner could get him to dry land in much quicker time.

> "City of Paris," Thursday, Feb. 20:—
> On deck part of the day but awful sick from morning till night. Did not eat anything at all. I don't see any pleasure in going to sea. I wish I was home. Why was I such a fool to leave home? The sea is black and ugly and the ship rolls and pitches. Mr. Hunt has crossed 12 times but says he never saw anything like this. Last night everything movable in our cabin broke

from their fastenings and in the morning we felt
we had been pounded all over.

Saturday:—Pulled on my waterproof ulster
and managed to get up on deck. It was the
grandest sight I ever saw. The waves were
mountains high, fifty feet I should say by actual
measurement. These great waves toss our ship
about as if it was made of cork. I am getting very
weak and unless I eat soon I shall starve to
death.

Sunday:—The sea is calmer but still I can't eat.

Monday:—A fine bright day and the sea comparatively calm. I'm still starving.

Tuesday, 10 P.M.:—We just passed Fastnet
Light and are in the Irish sea. Everything is
calm and my sickness is gone. Have forgotten
how sick I was already.

Woolworth landed in Liverpool and went immediately to Staffordshire to select pottery.

Stoke on Trent, Staffordshire, England,
                    Saturday, March 1, 1890:
I can eat now and never was so hungry in my
life. This is the centre of the potteries, over 600
of them in the County of Staffordshire. Some of
the finest china in the world is made here and
some of the poorest. We have been in over 25
potteries the last three days and have not bought
anything yet, but expect to next week. There are
no stoves but open fire places and at night we all
sit around them. . . . I am getting to be quite an
Englishman and can eat Gorgonzola cheese,
Stilton cheese, marmalade, cauliflower, mutton,
pot pie, plum pudding, and several other
luxuries. Cheese I eat every meal, same as the

rest do. It is brought in in about 50 pound pieces and everyone digs out what he likes of it and in that way it is always fresh. No one is in a hurry here. We go to bed by candles in huge silver candlesticks. The shops, we cannot call them stores, are very small and dark as a pocket. They have no street cars but tram cars run by a dummy steam engine. The cars are two story and are plastered over with advertisements.

A postscript to this letter, by Mr. Hunt, mentions that Woolworth weighs 187 pounds. Woolworth describes another experience in Staffordshire:

Stoke on Trent, March 4:—

We went today to a hotel for dinner and ate in what they call "The Ordinary." It cost us two and three pence (56 cents) and is patronized mostly by commercial men or travelers. The first thing they do is elect a President who must be the oldest patron of the hotel, not in age but according to the length of time he has stopped there. He sits at the head of the table and is the Carver, and the Vice President sits at the foot of the table and is his assistant carver. Today there were 16 at the table. First they brought on the soup and then about 50 pounds of roast beef, and set it before the President, and some roast mutton, and placed it before the Vice President, and when all is ready the President says to the Vice: "Mr. Vice, will you assist me in serving the gentlemen?" And he responds yes and they get down to business. The roast beef was the finest I ever ate. After that course was over they served puddings in the same way and then cheese, as Englishmen nearly always finish up on

cheese. After all are through the waiter comes
around with a silver plate and collects the two
shillings, three pence, commencing with the
President, after which the President thanks us
very kindly and all is over. It is a very nice
custom and I wonder it has never been introduced in America.

The travelers next visited London, which Woolworth describes:

London, Wednesday, March 5, 1890:—
Our first impression of London was not very
exalted, although the day was as fine as they ever
get in London. The whole city is covered with a
dense smoke caused by using soft coal, and re-
minds one of Pittsburgh before the reign of natural gas. The low dingy buildings are black with
it, and we were somewhat disappointed with
the Largest City in the World. We took a carriage to the Hotel Savoy, an entirely new hotel
and considered one of the finest in the world.
We dined in a fashionable restaurant on the
Strand.
A fine orchestra discoursed fine music while
we ate. Dress suits for Gents and Ladies is the
rule there, but of course we had none to wear.
The ladies wear very low neck dresses in all
public places here in the evenings, and we soon
got accustomed to them. We went to the Lyceum
Theatre and saw Henry Irving and Ellen Terry
play the "Dead Heart."
The streets of London are very interesting to
a foreigner. They may have some fine stores here
but we have not yet found them. Those we have
seen are nothing but little shops and the way

they trim their windows is new to me. They trim
them close to the glass from the top to the bottom, and it is impossible to look into the store.
The stores themselves are very small and are
called "shops" and not much like our fine stores.
I think a good penny and six pence store run by
a live Yankee would create a sensation here, but
perhaps not. I have not been in a single store or
place where I am obliged to speak but they spot
me for an American, and they try to sell me goods
that demand a high duty. It is almost impossible
to understand some of these Englishmen, they
talk so different from us, and they have hard
work to understand us sometimes. Mr. Hunt took
me into the Bar Room of the Grand Hotel, which
was fitted up fine, and behind the bars, dealing
out liquids of all kinds, were handsome Bar Maids
dressed up in the height of fashion, as this is
the custom in all bar rooms in England, large
or small, to have female bartenders. The people
on the street have not got the life and bustle
New York City people have, and you can hardly
realize you are in a very large city. The buildings
are very low as compared to New York, and we
very seldom see one over five stories high.

And again:

London, March 6:—
This forenoon we spent buying goods such as
scrap books, albums, etc and took lunch in a
restaurant in the Old Palace of Richard the
Third in the Throne Room. The bill of fare was
dated 1466 but the meats and vegetables are
comparatively modern. We then visited the
House of Parliament, or at least looked at it

from the outside, and Westminster Abbey which I consider the greatest sight in London. The guard at the door would not let me pass until I opened up my Kodak and proved to him there was no dynamite in it. They were holding services at the time and we had a chance to hear the great Organ, and I never heard such a fine toned organ before . . .

Mr. Hunt and Woolworth next went to Germany:

Frankfort on the Main, Germany,
Friday, March 7:—
We left London at 8.30 P.M. last night and went by rail to Queensborough and took a steamer across the North Sea to Flushing in Holland where we arrived at 7 A.M. this morning and of all the mean rotten accommodations we have had on our trip those we had on the steamer were the worst. Although we took first class we were dumped into a so-called State Room with four coffin shaped boxes to rest our weary bones on. But we passed the night some way and had our first rotten meal at Flushing. I did not eat it. You all know my weakness for good victuals and can appreciate my situation. To add to the horrors everyone was talking Dutch and even Mr. Hunt could not understand it. A few minutes after we landed we were off for Germany and passed for miles over a level country until we came to the German frontier at 11.30 A.M., where all our baggage was examined by a lot of German officials in gold lace, with a pompous bearing. They went through my trunk and found a celluloid case with brushes, etc., that Miss Creighton gave me for Christmas that looked

too new to them, and a few linen collars. They made me pay the enormous duty of five pfennigs or 1⅓ cents just to show their authority. We got to Cologne at one o'clock and had to wait an hour and a half for another train, and got a good dinner at depot there, and spent the rest of the time at the Great Cathedral, one of the finest in Europe. We arrived in Frankfort about 8 P.M. and found a beautiful city of about 150,000 and a fine hotel, last but not least good square meals and fine bedrooms heated with steam. All the buildings we saw were fine and bore quite a contrast to smoky London, with a bright clear air. The only drawback was we could not speak their language and were obliged to depend upon Mr. Hunt entirely, and hung to him like a child for fear of getting lost. The ride from Cologne to Frankfort was for the most part of it along the banks of the historic and beautiful River Rhine. The scenery is perfectly beautiful, more so than our famous Hudson River.

Next Woolworth and Hunt went to buy dolls at Sonneberg:

On our arrival at Sonneberg the whole town was there to meet Mr. Hunt, as he is a great favorite here for several reasons. One is that he buys more dolls than any other importer that comes into Sonneberg and another is he makes friends wherever he goes. After the handshaking, kissing, etc., were all over, we took the bus to Krug's Hotel where we shall stay several days. Sonneberg is headquarters for dolls for the whole world, as nearly every doll of every description is made here or within a few miles from here, and this is the market. It is a place of about 15,000 people.

March 9:—

It seems as though the whole toy trade of America is represented here. As we walked along the street we could look in the windows of the houses and see the women and children at work making dolls, while the men drink beer. Nearly every doll is made in private houses. We could see some of the women and children molding the legs, others the head, some putting the hair on, another making the shirts, others putting in the eyes, and one would be painting the finished doll. After they are finished they are put in long baskets and taken to the packers where they are put into boxes of one dozen each and put into large cases and shipped to all parts of the world. The poor women do most of the work even to lugging them to the packing houses.

March 14:—

It is no longer a mystery to me how they make dolls and toys so cheap, for most of it is done by women and children at their homes anywhere within 20 miles of this place. Some of the women in America think they have got hard work to do, but it is far different than the poor women here, that work night and day on toys, and strap them onto their backs, and go 10 or 20 miles through the mud with 75 pounds on their backs, to sell them. The usual price they get for a good 10 cent doll is about 3 cents each here, and they are obliged to buy the hair, shirts and other materials, to put them together, and they probably get about 1 cent each for the labor they put on them.

The streets are filled with women with baskets on their backs filled with dolls and toys, and they walk in the middle of the street when the mud is ankle deep in preference to the clean sidewalk. We saw a poor little girl that could not have been over four years old with a basket strapped on her back larger than herself and Mr. Hunt asked her where she lived and she told us a place about five miles from here, and she came alone. We gave her some money and she looked at it as if she never saw any of it before. It is an ordinary thing here to see a dog and a woman hitched together or cows and women drawing a heavy load of goods.

We can find out more about the toy and china business of America here than at home. Here we find out what the other firms are buying and what they pay for the goods. I have found out where these Sailor Dolls that we sold so many of are made here and we can save considerable by buying them direct. We have also struck a firm where a certain house in Philadelphia gets a big line of toys that we have bought for several years. Nearly all the dealers on this side tell us who they sell to in America. I am trying to learn German but it is a very hard language to learn. I go out in the stores once in a while alone and have had no trouble to get what I wanted. I came very near being thrown out of a window in one sample room while I was trying to get off my Dutch, as I told the man he was no good without knowing the meaning. Since then I have been very careful. They all have great sport with me trying to learn, but I don't care, but keep at it every day. . . . You will notice I do not enthuse very much over the cooking since I left England.

I cannot say that I have had what I call a good square meal since we left the Savoy Hotel in London.

March 17:—

This has been a very fine day and we went to a small place on the cars among the mountains called Lanscha to buy Christmas tree ornaments. The scenery was very fine. Lanscha is noted for the manufacture of marbles and Christmas tree ornaments. The manufacture of marbles was very interesting to us. The cheap painted marbles that cost in America 45 cts. per thousand we saw manufactured. Each marble is painted by hand and goes through the hands of three different girls, just painting alone, and they get 3 cents per thousand for painting them. Glass marbles are made in a different way, the striped or "all fine" marbles are all made of glass and the colors are put in about the same as in stick candy, and rolled around and left to cool. Tree ornaments are made out of blown glass, and the quicksilver is put inside afterwards. They are made by the very poorest class there is in Europe and we were obliged to go into their dirty hovels to see what we could use. One place we went into we found a man and a woman in one room with six small children, the youngest not over eight years old, and both man and woman hard at work. It was the dirtiest and worst smelling place I was ever in, but they seemed to be happy in their filth and dirt. How they could live was a mystery to me and this was only a sample of hundreds of houses in Lanscha. Out of 4,000 population there, Mr. Hunt says 3,500 of them are under 5 years of age. How true that is I am unable to tell but I never saw so many children

in my life in so small a town. The streets are
full of them and most of them barefooted and
bareheaded and the snow not all off the ground
yet. We waded through mud ankle deep up hill
and down in search of marbles and tree ornaments all day. We took dinner at a hotel called
in English "Hotel of the Wild Man" and the
proprietor did his best to feed us, and succeeded,
more or less. We took possession of the hotel
for two or three hours . . . and we all danced
except Mr. Hunt (my first attempt). We made
the old hotel tremble, and frightened the natives.
I do think a livelier crowd never struck the town.

From Sonneberg, Woolworth made a trip through
the mountains of Saxony to Gotha, which he describes:

Gotha, Saxony, March 21:— We left a comparatively warm climate and by the time we got
on top of the mountains we found about six
inches of snow, and quite cold. The ride was
quite the most romantic of any we have had.
Talk about the Horse Shoe Bend, Mauch Chunk
or Hudson River scenery, it is no comparison
to what we saw on this ride up the mountain. On
the top of this mountain we find the largest manu-
factures of toy tea sets in the world, and were
treated in royal style. The proprietor lent us his
team, carriage and coachman to visit all factories.
Nearly every sample room we have been in has
been so cold we could hardly stand it, but we
struck one here that was very hot and we got
thoroughly warmed through and through and
then came out into the night air and went to our
hotel and went to bed in the coldest room we

have struck yet. They did not give us a sheet or a blanket to cover over us but instead we got a feather tick full of feathers, which is the style in all Germany. In cold weather, if you lie still and do not move until morning, you can manage to keep warm, but if you move around very much the feathers will work down on either side. Don't think many newly married couples come to Germany to spend their honeymoons, for there is not such a thing as a double bed in the whole country.

Then Woolworth visited the quaint old walled city of Nuremberg, a toy center, and Munich, where he enjoyed the beer, the opera and the art museums. He took a trip alone to Vienna for Easter Sunday and was entranced with the beauty and gaiety of the Austrian capital.

Vienna, Sunday April 6:—

Vienna, beautiful, magnificent Vienna, words cannot express the beauties of this city. I had heard much about Vienna being a beautiful city, but did not realize it was so magnificent. Such artistic and fine buildings all over the city, such fine statuary on every side, such fine carvings, and works of art must be seen to be appreciated. I cannot describe them. And the elegant coffee houses, the finest bread and rolls in the world and last, but not least, the handsomest girls of any city in the world. They are one of the sights of the city and one can scarcely see on the streets an ordinary looking girl and as for real homely girls they are impossible to find. The streets are paved with stone and asphalt and are so clean you could eat your dinner off them. The store windows make the finest display of any city I was ever in. Everything looks so new and odd, and very tempting. It is all I can do to keep my money in my pocket. "The Graba" is the great retail street and is thronged continually from 8 in the morning until 8 at night. The proper time for ladies to go shopping is between 4 and 8 P.M., and that is the time to see the people. Not only the ladies dress and look fine, but the men are elegantly dressed with silk hats, gloves and canes. You see no dudes on the street but sensible looking business men and it hardly seems possible among such fine looking, intelligent people that not one in a thousand can speak a word of English, though they look more like Americans than in any city we have been in. . . . My first impression of Vienna was rather strange, arriving here at 10 o'clock at night. The moon was shining brightly and I could see the fine buildings, and saw they were above the average in beauty, but the streets were practically deserted, as it is the custom to go home at 8 or 9 o'clock and, after that time, there is no life here. It being Good Friday all the art galleries were closed up but had enough to see just the same. Visited several fine churches that were simply grand and must have cost a mint of money. In the afternoon took a drive out of the city to the Emperor's Summer Palace. The walls in each room are very artistically decorated in white and gold and nearly all hung in paintings, not hung in frames but painted on the wall itself. Even the ceilings are covered with paintings. In the Emperor's bedroom saw the original bed that Napoleon First slept in when he occupied the Palace after he had taken the city. Napoleon must have been a perfect terror to all of Europe in his time, as we see his works nearly every place we go. . . . I never saw such good coffee before. It comes with a rich thick foam on top which seems to be the secret of its flavor. And the beautiful rolls that Vienna boasts cannot be beat. . . . Today being Easter Sunday visited several churches and the special music was grand to hear. Every church has a regular orchestra and large chimes. Saw the old Emperor himself in his carriage. He is an ordinary looking man about sixty. The Imperial Opera House is the finest inside I ever saw. It has five galleries and nearly every one of them divided off in boxes. Saw three different performances the same night. The first was "The Village Barber" and the next "The Doll's Fair" which I think has been played in New York. The last play was in pantomime, representing the four seasons, spring, summer, autumn and winter, and was simply immense.

April 7:—

Today I went to the Belvidere Picture Gallery owned by the Emperor and saw the works of Rubens, Rembrandt, Michael Angelo, Raphael, Durer and many other old masters. But I must say as a whole I cannot appreciate the famous works of the old masters as well as the modern pictures, with the exception of the pictures of Rubens' first and second wives, painted by himself, and a few others, including two famous pictures painted by Danner over 200 years ago representing an old man and an old woman. Each is about 12 by 18 inches and the Emperor was offered by some Englishman 250,000 pounds ($1,250,000) for them. They are certainly wonderful works of art and we are allowed to examine them very closely and I never saw anything more natural. It looks as if they could speak and the wrinkles in their faces, the veins, the tints on the cheeks and the beard of the old men, in fact the finest particles and pores of the skin are visible as though they were alive. Visited the park and saw Vienna out for a holiday. A finer dressed or well behaved class of people cannot be found and the man who takes Vienna for an old fashioned backwoods sort of place will get left badly. Children were playing with their nurses and by the way you should see the bright and gaudy colors the nurses wear, with dresses only to their knees, with red stockings and low shoes on, and nearly all wear hoops or something to make their dresses stick out all around like a ballet girl. We meet strange sights in every town and this city is a regular kaleidescope. Oh, if I could only stay here longer, but no use, I must go tonight sure, but I am in hopes of coming back again.

Woolworth left Vienna with a sigh and rejoined Mr. Hunt in Bohemia to buy vases and glass goods. The weather turned cold and rainy and he was glad to leave in three days for Dresden and the great annual Leipsic Fair:—

Leipsic, April 14:
Get out of the way, hustle up, tumble up, confusion. That is Leipsic during the Fair. Leipsic is a city of 150,000 inhabitants but now there is over 100,000 strangers here. They call it a Fair but it is not like our Fairs. Thousands of manufacturers from all over the world rent rooms

as near the heart of the city as possible, at very
high prices, and bring samples of their goods
here for sale.

April 17:

If any one likes hard work and lots of it,
let them come here and look over samples all
day, up and down stairs, jostled about in the
crowded streets, halls and sample rooms. Every
room from cellar to garret is a sample room.
While in Sonneberg I gave a large order (over
1,500 gross) for Christmas tree ornaments and
I am pointed out on every corner of the street
as the big buyer of tree ornaments and they
tackle me everywhere trying to sell me more. . . .
I will leave Mr. Hunt in Berlin tomorrow and go
on to Paris alone.

The next stop was Berlin, where Woolworth caught
glimpses of royalty.

Grand Hotel De Rome, Berlin, April 19:—
We arrived in this handsome city last night at
9.15 from Leipsic. Visited the Royal Palace this
forenoon and the National Gallery this afternoon.
One of the great sights in Berlin are the soldiers.
Today the soldiers were all called out to salute
the Empress as she was passing by in her carriage and nearly every person took off their hats
except myself. I could see no sense in such nonsense. . . . Today I wandered into a show of
waxed figures and while looking at a tattooed
girl heard her drop a few words of English. She
told me she was an American and had come to
London with Barnum's show and will show in
the various cities of Europe.

Berlin, April 20:—

A lot of letters from home were thrown on my bed before I was up today and I read them before I got up. Don't know how many copies of these letters Mr. Peck sends out but I shall remember all those who have written me, also those who have not written. Sales I see are all ahead of last year. Mr. Peck has grasped the situation very quick and taken my place in the New York office in fine shape. When reading these long letters don't forget the immense amount of work it makes Miss Holahan in reading my miserable writing and copying them for you with Mr. Ivie's help. It seems impossible to read some of them myself for they have been written on the cars, by candle-light and under all circumstances whenever I could catch a moment's time. Have been away two months and have had no strawberries, celery, oranges, no beans, buckwheat cakes, oysters; but they have lots of dishes here we don't. I have a good appetite and can eat most anything but draw the line at sausage and caviar. The latter is composed of fish eggs, raw, soaked in oil and looks like black tea. This afternoon Mr. Hunt and I took a walk on the "Unter Den Linden" and heard a great commotion and rolling of drums and soldiers presenting arms and thousands of people rushing to the centre of the street and a fine carriage coming at full speed drawn by four elegant horses and plumes and footmen in fine livery, and in the carriage was the Emperor himself seated by the side of a lady. He is very young looking and had on a brass helmet hat and fine uniform. It was a sight to see the people take off their hats and bow. Tonight we go to see Verdi's new opera, "Othello."

After parting with Mr. Hunt in Berlin, Woolworth set out for Paris. While on the train Woolworth wrote:

Last night the first Frenchmen came into the car I was in and I listened very attentively and managed to learn one very important word Oui (wee) which means yes in French.

Although at first disappointed, Woolworth rapidly became captivated with Paris:

Grand Hotel De-l-Athenee, Paris,
Thursday, April 24:—
My first impression of Paris was disappointing. We drove down an ordinary street for a mile or so to the hotel and I says to myself Can this be Paris we hear so much about? The buildings are low and looked smoked up and not many people on the street. After paying the cab fare etc., I had only two francs left and in a strange city over 3,000 miles from home and I did not know a word of French. But all this did not worry me in the least and I put on as much cheek as I would have done with a thousand francs in my pocket. The first hard work I did was to order a Table De Hote dinner. After dinner, I took a walk; then and not until then I began to see the beauties of Paris. It looks more like New York than any European city I have been in. Nearly all the men wear silk hats and gloves. In the evening dress suits are the rule. If I ever come to Europe again I shall not leave

my silk hat at home and will surely bring a dress suit. Paris is New York enlarged on a grand scale and is a very gay city. I don't know what the people do for a living, it seems to be all pleasure and no work. The forenoon was rather disagreeable and rainy but it allowed me to see how the Parisian women expose their small feet and ankles. Indeed, they take delight in exposing more than the ankles. Nearly every one of them when the streets are wet carry their overskirts over their arms. This afternoon I spent two hours in the famous Louvre Picture Gallery and saw some of the most famous paintings of the world. Rubens must have been a hard worker for he seems to have more paintings in Europe than any other painter. Paris is too much to see in a minute or a day and I am completely paralyzed with so much to see.

Paris, April 25:—

The more one sees of Paris, the more magnificent it looks and there seems to be no limit to its grandeur. The cabs here are very cheap. You can ride anywhere in the city from point to point for one and a half francs (30 cents) but the driver will call out "Poor Boy" which in English means a fee. Today visited the Luxemburg and enjoyed the modern paintings and the statuary more than the old ones at the Louvre. Saw the Pantheon and rode up the famous boulevard Champs-Elysees to the Arc de Triomphe and saw Napoleon's Tomb.

Paris, April 26:—

This afternoon I visited the world famous store "The Bon Marche" which is probably the largest store in the world. They employ 4,000

people regular and feed them all in the same
building. It is as near like Wanamaker's store
in Philadelphia as any store I know of but on a
much larger scale. On the busy days the sales
would run up to 1,500,000 francs ($300,000).
They use no cash system whatsoever but each
customer must go to the desk and pay for what
they buy. They are not allowed to pay the clerks
who wait on them, a system that would not work
in America.

Paris, April 27:—

Last night went to the opera "Faust." The
Opera House itself is indescribably beautiful.
Today drove all around sight-seeing, the Bois de
Boulogne, the chief park of the French capital,
etc. While in the Cathedral of Notre Dame heard
the large organ and some very fine singing. Spent
several hours in the old Royal Palace, the oldest
building in France, built in 200. Suppose you
know the French people are the best cooks in the
world. It is wonderful how tempting and nice
everything is as it is brought on to the table.
All the words I know in French are yes, no,
waiter and thank you, besides knowing how to
count up to twelve, but tonight I made up my
mind to go alone to a restaurant away from the
hotel (where they speak English). Well I managed to get soup, roast beef and coffee all right
but I wanted dessert and decided to go it blind.
I pointed out an article marked a franc and a
half and thought I could stand that all right. The
waiter brought me the finest strawberries I ever
saw, served with the stems on in very small jars,
containing about 5 strawberries each, and four
or five jars in a small box filled in with moss. . . .

I have not got the confidence in these French people I had in the Germans, for they will take the last cent a man has and call for more.

A week in Paris was all too brief. Then back to London, which this time seemed "homelike" and the British accent not so difficult. Woolworth had engaged passage on the steamship *Etruria*, sailing from Liverpool May 10; and he devoted the interim to renewed sightseeing in London and a quick trip to the potteries to make certain his orders had been filled.

The *Etruria* paused at Queenstown and Woolworth had an opportunity to step for the first time on Irish soil.

Queenstown, Sunday, May 11:—

Arrived here at five o'clock this morning and had to wait until noon for the arrival of the Royal Mail. All cabin passengers had a chance to go ashore. Four of us got into a jaunting cart to see the town. This is rightly named. We hung on with all our might while the driver whipped up his horse and cracked jokes for us, which he seemed to be as full of as a nut of meat. I asked him if he knew my Grandfather [Henry Mc-Brier] when he lived in Ireland. "Oh, yes, I knew him well. He was a foine man with strait hair, curley teeth and only one upper lip." At 1 P.M. our steamer started and at 5 we bade goodbye to land and Europe. The waves began to roll and the 1,300 stomachs on our good old ship and I bid goodbye to breakfast and lunch.

The homeward voyage was rough:

Monday: Stormy. Ate nothing. The day has been so long. Will it never come to an end?

Tuesday: A terrible hurricane with the sea boiling and foaming and big waves breaking over it. . . . This has been the longest and most disagreeable day I ever put in.

Wednesday: Sea calmer. Ate a little dinner but didn't enjoy it.

Friday: Have been able to go to meals for three days but the food doesn't seem natural.

However, the sands of Coney Island were soon in sight and this is the traveler's *l'envoi:*

Brooklyn, Sunday, May 18.

"Home Sweet Home" at last. It's almost worth the three months trip for the pleasure of this day alone. But New York does not look as large as it used to. . . . Such hugging and kissing I never got before. The only thing I had to pay duty on was three big dolls I got for my three children ($2.10). We finally got home at ten and had breakfast and no one told me the bad news of Mr. Hesslet's death until noon.[1]

At first it seemed impossible that one of the best friends I ever had should pass away so quickly. It seems he made out the reports of the Harrisburg store at 6 P.M. Thursday night and mailed them to the New York office and then took a ride on his bicycle and he was found dead by the side of the road and the doctors said it was heart failure. The funeral is to be in Lancaster

---

[1] H. H. Hesslet, Woolworth's partner in the Harrisburg, Pa., store, died suddenly of heart failure Thursday, May 15, while Woolworth was on the ocean.

tomorrow (Monday) and my wife and I will go there tonight . . .

As soon as I landed I asked Mr. Kirby where my brother was. And the reply was that he had been very busy in the past week and had succeeded in raising an 8 pound boy, and no doubt he feels very happy. Everything seemed to run smoothly under Mr. Peck. Before concluding I want to thank Mr. Ivie, my bookkeeper, and Miss Holahan, the typewriter, for the way they have copied and mailed my letters. I have tried to explain Europe as it looked to me. I will now bid you goodbye and trust if any of you ever go to Europe you will have as pleasant and as enjoyable a time as I have had.

Yours respectfully,

F. W. Woolworth.

In more ways than one, the European journey proved of immense value to Woolworth.

Chapter VII

A Million-Dollar Business

WOOLWORTH'S imagination needed no spur, but if it had his European trip would have provided the necessary fillip. Shortly after his return he astonished his managers with one of those provocative messages that were always dropping into their morning mail:

"I have been looking over a census of the United States and I am convinced that there are one hundred cities and towns where we can locate five-and-ten-cent stores and we can sell a million dollars' worth of goods a year!"

The great tide of immigration to the United States was just setting in, and during more than a quarter of a century thereafter the growth of population was a study which absorbed Woolworth as a hobby. He maintained elaborate charts which revealed to him how towns and cities were growing. As the curve of immigration rose, so did the curve of his ambition. The immigrants would be his customers! All those millions with very little money could afford to trade at the five-and-tens, even the poorest.

In adding to his chain, he proceeded with his usual caution and care. After opening two stores in Massachusetts, at Springfield and Worcester, he made his first venture into the South, at Richmond, Virginia. This Southern invasion was launched with some misgivings, but these were soon dispelled. The Richmond store surprised him gratifyingly by establishing two new records. The total of the first day's sale was $821.50. The first week the total was $3,276.10. The store swarmed with Negro as well as white customers, the former doting particularly upon cosmetics and rainbow-hued imitation jewelry. So within three months he opened another Virginia store, in Norfolk; and this, too, on opening day was aswarm with eager buyers.

Then in the summer of 1891, following another European trip, Woolworth launched his most ambitious venture.

When he had started out a dozen years before to find a location for his first five-cent store, Rochester, New York, had been one of the places explored. At that time he had been unable to find space under $700 a year rental, and that alone had been sufficient to frighten him out. Ever since he had looked longingly toward Rochester.

Now, Woolworth decided to take the bull by the horns. He went to Rochester, scouted the business district and closed a lease for a store at 114 and 116 East Main Street for three years and eight months. The rent was $4,500 a year.

"We have the biggest store in the biggest city in the Syndicate," Woolworth informed his dubious associates. "Our location is prime. The store is large enough and the city big enough (138,000) to beat all records. We shall try to open three weeks from Saturday, August 22."

Three hectic weeks followed. Woolworth sent for his veteran helpers: Carson Peck from New York, Moore from Watertown, Gibbs from Utica, and Mrs. Coons from Syracuse. All worked like beavers. Center counters were built running the entire length of the store. The latest model cash system, with sixteen stations operated by pulleys, was installed; and five great arc lights. Sixty clerks were hired and coached.

Woolworth and his aides awaited the opening with the eagerness of actors behind a first night's curtain. Each placed estimates as to the first day's sales in sealed envelopes, with a ten-dollar bill as reward for the best guess. All estimates proved too low. The opening was a triumph. Sales up to noon were $207.57; noon to 6 P.M., $477.15; 6 P.M. to 11 o'clock closing, $434.50—a grand total of $1,119.22. For the first time a five-and-ten had sold more than $1,000 worth of goods in a single business day! Woolworth broadcast the historic news in a boastful bulletin.

"We are the talk of the town," he trumpeted. "All wonder how we can pay such rent and sell goods so cheap. It is safe to say the first day's sales record will never be broken. We had customers from the moment we opened until we closed. In the evening there must have been over 500 people in the store-at once and the heat and smell was awful."

Rochester rolled up an unprecedented seven-day sales' record of $5217.95.

The following spring three small stores were opened, in Bethlehem, Pa., Holyoke, Mass., and Paterson, N. J.

The year 1893 opened with dark clouds over the business world. Like all good orthodox Republicans, Woolworth shook his head sadly over the election of Grover Cleveland and predicted dire things for the country. By the end of the year, breadlines had lengthened and the streets of every large city were filled with shelterless and unemployed men. The starving jobless could only howl while Carnegie and other big shots blandly demanded and obtained tremendous tariff support for their struggling "infant" industries.

The panic of '93 struck deeply. Hundreds of firms collapsed. The comparatively young Woolworth Syndicate was fortunate in the soundness of its structure. It had no outstanding debts or debtors, and ample cash reserves. Though the panic hit its sales somewhat, this loss was offset by a drop in wholesale prices. In fact, the Woolworth dime stretched further than it ever had before; and for the first time Woolworth was able to add suspenders, belts, pocketbooks, and many other articles to his sales list.

In 1894—the year of Coxey's Army, the Pullman strike and an almost bankrupt federal treasury—the five-and-ten reached a new high in sales: $880,418.23.

During this depressed period, Woolworth used the bulk of his capital to buy goods at the low prices. However, he was able to open eight new stores in three years. One was in Newark, N. J., where nine years before Woolworth & Knox had failed. This time the story was different, the first day's sales reaching a new high mark of $1807.55.

Thus, by the spring of 1895, five-and-ten had not only weathered the panic, but in the course of five years had doubled its stores and tripled its sales.

There were now twenty-eight stores listed under the Diamond ⬥Ⓦ which Woolworth has adopted as his trade-mark. Eight were in New York, six in Pennsylvania, five in New Jersey, three in Massachusetts, two each in Connecticut and Virginia, while Delaware and New Hampshire contained one apiece.

Yearly sales had grown to well over a million dollars a year.

These were all Woolworth's own stores; and for the most part in charge of salaried managers. By now, Woolworth had ample capital and was able to control his business. Each manager, however, was given a wide latitude in the detailed operation of his individual store. He could order goods according to the needs of his trade; though he was expected to push new items as directed from headquarters, he did not have to reorder unless trade justified it. The most potent stimulus to the manager was a bonus plan permitting him participation in the net profits of his store up to 25 per cent. However, this arrangement demanded great care in the selection of store heads. Time and again Woolworth went back to Watertown for his men, men who had been reared in the same rugged school as himself and whose backgrounds he knew.

Clinton P. Case, the former Watertown drygoods clerk, was first placed in charge of the Rochester store, then brought to the New York office as assistant buyer. Case's successor in Rochester was none other than Harry Moody, the young clerk with whom Woolworth had slept in Bushnell's basement sixteen years before. Two more five-and-ten millionaires in the making. Clarion B. Winslow was another Watertown find.

Nor did Woolworth overlook his in-laws. In addition to his favorite sister-in-law, Mary Ann Creighton, the pioneer woman manager, Mrs. Woolworth's two younger brothers, Henry and Al, were put in charge of stores and a younger sister, Henrietta, was employed in the New York office. Woolworth's own cousin, Herbert G., was placed in the Bridgeport, Conn., store as assistant manager.

Constantly on the alert for promising men among his managers to strengthen his New York staff, Woolworth brought B. W. Gage from Wilmington to New York and gave him the resounding title of buyer and construction superintendent. Gage's store had long been noted for its attractiveness. He had a knack, second only to Woolworth's, for arrangement and display. In his new post his function was to make every store in the syndicate as attractive as possible and uniform in appearance.

However, in the spring of 1892, through the medium of a five-cent newspaper ad, Woolworth hired a youth destined to become his most valued lieutenant.

This was Hubert Templeton Parson, nineteen, a native of Toronto, Canada. With some knowledge of bookkeeping and accountancy, young Parson was seeking his fortune in New York. At that time, as one of its many circulation schemes, Joseph Pulitzer's *New York World* was permitting ambitious, though presumably impecunious, job seekers to insert want ads for the modest sum of five cents. Parson invested a nickel. His small coin, as we shall see, yielded fabulous returns.

Woolworth, needing another bookkeeper, saw the advertisement, liked its tone and sent for the young man. The interview took place in Woolworth's new and larger office on the second floor, Chambers Street side, of the Stewart Building.

"What can you do for me?" Woolworth asked the youth with keen dark eyes and bushy brows.

"Anything you've got for me to do," replied Parson.

"All right," said Woolworth, "I'll try you. The pay will be eight dollars a week."

Parson asked if he might have a day to think over the offer, since he had another appointment with a prospective employer. The next day he returned and said that, though he had been offered the second position at more money, he preferred to work for Woolworth.

It was a fortunate decision for both men. Parson had a photographic memory. He was a genius at digesting and cataloguing details, and keeping them in finger-tip readiness. Soon, young Parson was doing so well with the books, that his predecessor, Alvin Ivie, was sent into the field, first as manager at Kingston, then in charge of the larger Albany store. Before long Ivie was joined by another former member of the New York office staff. In one of the chatty letters which Woolworth still wrote to his managers, he mentions an event which was about to take place at his home:

At 4 P.M. today at 209 Jefferson Avenue all that remains of Alvin E. Ivie, manager of the Albany store, and Miss Et Creighton, an ex-employee of the New York office, will be united in the Bans of Matrimony and will start immediately on their wedding trip. I understand there have been several bushels of rice ordered and there have been several men employed for a week collecting old shoes. There has been talk of an invisible wire stretched across the door of the room where they are to be married. A balky horse has been engaged to take them to the station. A card has been labeled "Bride and Groom" to hang on the rear of the carriage.

Meanwhile Woolworth traveled constantly over his circuit, dropping into stores unannounced, and woe betide the manager whose counters, shelves or windows were slovenly. To him the boss seemed ubiquitous. He particularly abhorred cheap and hasty window displays and would often jump in himself and decorate a window with tasty arrangements of artificial flowers, glassware and so on.

"On my last visit around to the stores," he wrote in late September, 1891, "I noticed clerks running all over the place waiting on customers. That's the country store way of waiting on people but it won't do for us. Give each girl a counter and let her stick to it. In one of the stores I saw a cashier reading a novel. This you should put a stop to at once and not allow any one to read or chew gum during business hours."

Early in December he began pepping up the boys for the holiday trade:

"Give your store a holiday appearance. Hang up Christmas ornaments. Perhaps have a tree in the window. Make the store look different. This is our harvest time. Make it pay. This is also a good time to work off 'stickers' or unsalable goods, for they will sell during the excitement when you could not give them away other times. Mend all broken toys and dolls every day. Also, watch your clerks and customers to see they do not steal. When the store is crowded, don't allow any boys or girls in the store at all, unless they are with their parents, as most of them come in on purpose to steal. The cashier also needs your watchful eye, as it has been the experience of at least one store every year to lose large amounts through the cashier's dishonesty. Remember, the cashier has the best chance of all to steal."

A recurrent problem was the question of wages.

In his first stores, as we have seen, Woolworth paid his girls $1.50 a week. At that time there had been few outlets for women save domestic service or the factory. But as women advanced in the business world and their numbers multiplied, so did their demands for better pay. The backwash of these demands hit Woolworth, who raised the pay of his clerks fractionally, fighting bitterly every increase.

Woolworth took up the issue in his annual letter of 1892.

"We pay out more than one third of our annual expenses for salaries," he wrote. "We must have cheap help or we cannot sell cheap goods. When a clerk gets so good she can get better wages elsewhere, let her go—for it does not require skilled and experienced salesladies to sell our goods. You can get good honest girls at from $2 to $3 per week and I would not give $3.50 for any saleslady except in special cases. It may look hard to some of you for us to pay such small wages but there are lots of girls that live at home that are too proud to work in a factory or do housework. They are glad of a chance to get in a store for experience if nothing more and when they get experience they are capable of going to a store which can afford to pay good wages. But one thing is certain: we cannot afford to pay good wages and sell goods as we do now, and our clerks ought to know it."

The Christmas season that year brought the five-and-ten's first organized labor trouble, with wages the issue. Woolworth wrote his managers on December 13, 1892:

"One store writes in that all their girls are on strike for higher wages. No doubt they take advantage now while we are so busy, and think we will pay the advance. All such girls you should remember when the dull season comes and give them the 'bounce'."

In his constant search for novelties there was little that the master mind of the five-and-ten overlooked.

In 1890 the box office of Tony Pastor's was besieged by crowds who wanted to hear stout Maggie Cline sing, "Down Went McGinty." A few will remember McGinty went to the bottom of the sea, but he also "went" as a toy balloon on counters of dime stores. There were also McGinty watches which Woolworth bought at $8.50 a gross.

Summers found the Woolworths in a cottage on the Jersey shore. And there were other evidences of growing opulence, including purchase of a carriage and pair. On July 2, 1894, the master of the five-and-ten wrote his men with apparent casualness: "I expect to

move my family and horses to Asbury Park tomorrow
and our address will be the same as last year, 1100
Grand Avenue . . ." That "and horses" was something
to make him glow with pride. The friends and employees who got this proof of how far he had traveled
had known him "when."

However, they all came together once a year for
a reunion, Woolworth designating the travel period
for which expenses could be charged. There were
smaller gatherings, too. Typical was a gathering of a
small part of the syndicate for a jolly get-together.
Woolworth insisted that his old boss, William H.
Moore, add a description of this occasion to the general letter:

"The first day the Ocean looked like any Ocean and
the thousands of nice looking people did not look any
better than our party and surely did not have any
more fun. The Razzle Dazzle, imitating a ship at sea,
was taken in, also Day's ice cream . . . the bathing is
piles of fun . . . the Girls don't look very much . . .
when they have bathing suits on. The suits they rent
are awful long and don't fit very good and the straw
hats are tough . . .

"Sunday—All went to church, walked, music, singing,
talking by the hour on Woolworth's fine piazza,
smoked and had lots of fun. Board walk . . . in the
evening.

"Tuesday—the 'Tally Ho' was ready, but it looked
like rain; four horses; darkey driver—darkey 2 with a
bugle. What music that darkey made with that thing.
The top . . . is made with a folding ladder . . . some
beautiful photographs of the ladies in graceful atti-
tudes making for the top seats . . . but what a gay
party . . . for a 28 mile drive down the beach."

These were old friends: Moore and Woolworth and
Carson Peck and Clinton Case and their women folks.

They were one big family. Sitting together on the porch or lolling on the beach, they exchanged office and personal gossip: the arrival of a baby in the home of Mr. and Mrs. Satterthwait of the Allentown store; the engagement of Allen Creighton and Miss Emma Harney of New Haven; and of Hubert Parson and Miss Maysie Gasque whose sister worked in the New York office.

There also, fanned by ocean breezes, Woolworth, Case, Peck and the others chatted of old days in Watertown—and planned still greater expansion for five-and-ten.

Chapter VIII

Invading the Big Cities

ON A STEAMING hot Saturday in August, 1895, with the thermometer 96 in the shade, Peck, Case and other executives of the Woolworth Syndicate found themselves in Washington, D. C. Their faces were anxious. For this was the opening day of the syndicate's twenty-ninth and most pretentious store, and for the first time the boss himself was not present.

Woolworth, who was buying goods in his old Bavarian stamping ground, had remained in Europe deliberately. He wanted to test the mettle of his men, to see what they could do without his guiding hand. So he had given them complete authority to remodel the large but dingy old drygoods store he had leased in the nation's capital in May before shepherding his wife and daughters on their first trip abroad. The remodeling had been expensive.

Woolworth, too, was anxious. But his misgivings were soon dispelled by a lyrical message from the Washington manager, J. H. Strongman:

"Once again the banner of Woolworth enterprise has been proudly unfurled to the winds of trade—Thou too, sail on, O emblem great, wave on, and keep thy place of state at the head of the Syndicate."

101

The same mail brought a more descriptive missive from Case.

"When I raised the sheet of paper covering the door my heart almost went out to the very end of my big toe," he wrote. "Great guns, what a mob! Women, darkies, police, enough to take the whole building and dump it into the Potomac River but we had to let them in. And they came like an Iowa cyclone and in less time than I can write the store was packed and we had to call on the police for help. All day a sweltering, perspiring crowd fought for bargains. The crush was so great that our glass side lights on both sides of the entrance were smashed. We took in $1,954.08, a new record."

Woolworth responded with a triple hurrah (by cable); doubled his purchases of German toys and dolls; and closed a deal to buy the entire output of a jackknife factory at a flat rate of eight cents a jackknife against a previous wholesale price of sixteen cents. Then he laid plans to snare nickels and dimes, millions upon millions of them, in every large city in the East.

The returned traveler had hardly stepped ashore in October, before he began prospecting in the business district of Brooklyn. The old City of Brooklyn had not yet been consolidated as a borough in the Greater City of New York. It was a vast, sprawling, rapidly growing community, or series of communities, the citadel of the middle class. Its largest retail stores, solid, conservative, dignified, were spread along Fulton Street in the vicinity of Flatbush Avenue.

Here Woolworth determined to make his bid. Emboldened by the success of the Washington venture, he leased a three-story-and-basement building, with ground-floor store space of 42 by 122 feet, on Fulton Street, three doors below Flatbush Avenue. The building was new, heated by steam and illuminated by arc lights.

On this establishment Woolworth and his boys spread themselves. The show windows contained side and rear plate glass mirrors. The interior woodwork was imitation mahogany, the center counters of hardwood cherry, felt covered, and the show cases of plate glass with mahogany frames illuminated with incandescent lights. There were four show cases for candy, three for jewelry. A new cable cash system was installed with two cups to each station, and twenty-four stations.

Huge placards announced the opening for Saturday, November 16, 1895; and promised hitherto unheard-of bargains. Public curiosity mounted, as did the gorge of some of the more conservative merchants of the neighborhood. Woolworth serenely invited the latter to a private reception and inspection the day before the opening—a new wrinkle. Most of them came.

A Brooklyn newspaper described the opening day: From the *Brooklyn Times:*

Collected A Crowd
Mr. F. W. Woolworth's New Venture Proves a Great Success

There was a big crowd outside the five-and-ten-cent store of F. W. Woolworth at 532 Fulton street at 9 o'clock this morning waiting for the doors to open and when they were, there was such a crush to get inside that three big policemen had more than their hands full in keeping the crowd in something like order. Even then the crush was so great that the crowd threatened several times to go through the big plate glass windows in front of the store.

The store is a novelty in Brooklyn and the

people were anxious to see what a big concern of the kind could sell for five and ten cents. The visitors were agreeably surprised when they found the big store stocked from floor to ceiling with useful and ornamental articles of almost every conceivable kind. The price in no instance went above the advertised limit—ten cents.

Mr. Woolworth had a force of 150 pretty girls on hand to attend to the wants of the customers and they had their hands full all day long with the thousands who called, for none of them went away without purchasing something.

The opening day's intake smashed all previous records—$3139.41.

Tired but triumphant, Woolworth went home that night and to bed, but not to sleep. At 2 A.M. the bell at 209 Jefferson Avenue rang furiously.

"Don't answer; burglars," whispered Mrs. Woolworth drowsily. But Woolworth stuck his head out of the window and discovered two of his out-of-town men and three girl volunteer helpers who had worked late in the new store and had been locked out of their boarding house. The Woolworths improvised couch-and-chair beds for them.

Incidentally, Mrs. Woolworth's capable sister, Mary Creighton, became manager of the Brooklyn store.

The year 1896 was a foreboding one for business. William J. Bryan and his free-silver followers were boldly challenging the financial autocracy of the industrial East. That fall Woolworth opened a store in Boston, in what he described as "the very best location," between the big store of R. H. White & Company and Jordan, Marsh Company. The five-and-ten man observed to his managers: "To show you how this silver craze [for free coinage of silver at a ratio of sixteen to one] affects rents, the rent for the store [Boston] as it reads in the lease is: 'annual rent of 52 pounds 4 ounces 17 pennyweights 12 grains of pure gold in coined money of the United States of America.' . . . there is nothing in this lease whatever which states how many dollars and cents it amounts to."

As Bryan's campaign progressed, Wall Street prophesied another period of panic and disaster. Prices dropped. This again produced a harvest for Woolworth: many new articles in tableware, kitchen utensils, textiles and so on came within his price range. Manufacturers hitherto aloof were now glad to do business with a man who could put cash on the line and buy in large quantities.

"If I had been willing to borrow, the business could have branched out much more rapidly," said Woolworth in later years. "But I stuck to my policy of paying cash and have never regretted it. I studied my daily sales sheets with great care. The result was we opened but four stores in 1896 and but six in 1897."

Among these stores, however, were Philadelphia, Boston, New York and Pittsburgh. All were instant money makers.

The pioneer Manhattan five-and-ten, opened in October, 1896, was located at 259 Sixth Avenue, near Seventeenth Street. For this two-story building Woolworth paid the unprecedented rental of $20,000 a year. It was in the hub of the retail district which was bounded, roughly, on the south and north by Fourteenth and Twenty-third streets and on the east and west by Broadway and Sixth Avenue. In this small area were concentrated most of New York's famous stores: Altman, Stern Brothers, Best & Co., Bonwit Teller, McCutcheon, Le Boutillier Brothers, James McCreery, and so on.

"The New York store"—as the pioneer was designated even after many others had been established in the Greater City—was on the shabby-genteel side of Sixth Avenue. Overhead the L trains puffed and coughed up red hot cinders which sometimes fell on unsuspecting heads. The New York store, however, did not create as resounding a splash as the Brooklyn invasion the previous year. Its customers, like those in the five-and-tens elsewhere, were overwhelmingly of the poorer classes, though occasionally curiosity or the bargain urge would bring well-dressed shoppers.

"We were still pretty much looked down on," recalls Alvin Ivie, who was given the management of the new store. "When upper-crusters who knew each other would meet, each would pretend to the other that it was her first visit to the store—even though I'd seen both at our counters repeatedly. Lace was a new line with us and we sold a lot of it."

Woolworth, too, had his eye out for the "upper-crusters." He wrote his managers:

"Be especially attentive to customers who come to your store in carriages. This class of people likes to be petted and waited upon. Managers should never smoke or wear their hats. Salesladies should be neat and clean and dressed in black."

Fred M. Woolworth, F. W.'s young third cousin, was made Ivie's assistant. Fred's brother, Herbert G., was learning the business in C. S. Woolworth's Scranton store. It is interesting to note the varying fate of these two brother cousins. Herbert was to branch out on his own, with disastrous results; Fred to remain with F. W., and ultimately be able to count his wealth in eight figures.

Other men, too, were climbing the Woolworth ladder. One was Harry Moody, the old Bushnell basement chum, who was assigned to the New York office to assist Case in buying European goods.

Another, Charles C. Griswold, a New York State farmer's son, who had made a striking success of the Norfolk, Va., store, was given the post, newly created, of traveling store inspector. His duty was to visit each store at least twice a year and turn in detailed suggestions and criticism. He became the organization's first efficiency expert. Soon the boys in the field were calling him Old Eagle Eye, and they grew to dread his reports and Woolworth's scathing and trenchant comments.

Here is a typical Griswold report, selected at random:

Big improvement in the condition of the stock in the basement; goods were being put in excellent condition. One defective electric wire. It was fixed. Snow was melting on the sidewalk and commencing to drip through on the 10 ct. hardware. Illustrates that a manager's eyes must be everywhere. Found a fire pail half empty. Manager says cats drink out of it.

Glass and mirrors clean but the shades on the lights were an exception. The candy girl wore one of the dirtiest aprons I'd seen for some time and her hair looked like "sloppy weather." Candy display looked more attractive than on previous visit. At jewelry case found lots of pains had been taken with the case but wouldn't call the trim effective. Some goods tarnished; different kinds of goods were not shown together. Counter display: too many goods in some boxes, not enough in others. Yet counters show a big improvement.

Store has about the right number of clerks for present business. Signs on the backs of counters were uneven, looked like the "Rocky Road to Dublin." Cash registers were running way off;

cashier not balancing them correctly. Manager had not noticed this. Store well lighted.

Sundries being watched very closely. General letter books not locked up. No rates given on freight bills. Any manager can demand and get this from the railroad company. Manager was not checking yellow slips with the bills when they came in. One of the yard measures tacked on the counter was 3½ inches too long.

On the whole, though, think this manager has done very well.

And Woolworth's comment:

Glad to learn there is improvement in this particular store. Also glad the inspector called the manager's attention to the untidy appearance of the candy girl. I wish to impress every manager to put the neatest, cleanest and most attractive girls behind your candy counter, as it surely helps to increase the sales. The manager gives a weak excuse when he says cats drink out of the fire pails. Always keep them full. The bad condition of the jewelry case should never be tolerated in any store. And signs at the back of the counter should be kept nice and straight.

What's the matter that the cash registers do not run right? What's the use of having a cashier unless she balances them up correctly? Why does the manager allow the general letter books to remain where persons that ought not can see them? These books and all private matters should be kept under lock and key. We hear too much about the secrets of our business leaking out.

So the yard measure on the counter was 3½ inches too long. I didn't suppose there was a single manager in our Syndicate who is ignorant of how many inches it takes to make a yard, yet this manager has been giving 39½ inches of goods for the price of 36. Now I want every manager at once to see that he has absolutely the correct measurements marked off on the back of the counter. For if you have been giving short measure you are liable to be jacked up by the sealers of weights and measures; and if you have been giving too much you have taken all the profits away from the goods.

The discovery of a wasted penny in his business never failed to irritate Woolworth, even when he had become fabulously rich. Waste in operations was treason to five-and-ten. Consequently, any Woolworth executive anywhere was trained to be careful with postage stamps, wrapping paper, twine, electric lights. The last man out of any room, though it was the boss himself, turned out the lights.

Woolworth would interrupt discussion of weighty matters to write this rebuke: "We received the following letters this morning with postage due, from Bethlehem—2 cts due, Paterson—4 cts due, and Utica sent in a letter with a 5 cent stamp on. Please study up postal laws again, and weigh your letters . . . if you have to pay anything on our letters let us know."

Nor in his constant effort to find new manufacturers with whom he could deal directly, did Woolworth overlook a chance to pick up old lots or bankrupt stocks for his counters. Indeed, he found excitement in this search such as other men find in the chase after big game.

"Today," he would inform his managers, "I made up my mind to find some bargains if possible . . . and I have succeeded although it was awful hard work . . .

thermometers on wood, imported, $7.50 per gross."
Or again he might turn up a lot of crockery "thirds"
including "large soup tureens, oval dishes, sugar bowls,
tea pots, chambers etc. The last item should be a
'corker'."

On another occasion he unearthed a lot of 2500
books at four cents each. Their titles included: *Tom
Brown at Rugby, The Terrible Temptation, The
Abbott, Old Mortality, Flying Dutchman, Old Si's
Humorous Sketches, The Monastery, The Antiquary,
The Wrong Man, The Shadows of the Bar, Waverley,
The Lion's Share, The Pomfret Mystery, Grandfather's
Chair, Red Gauntlet, Old Curiosity Shop, Billy's
Mother.* These made first-rate bargains.

All down the line economy was the watchword.
When the New York banks began charging one-tenth
of one per cent for collection on out-of-town checks,
the Woolworth account was transferred to the Fourth
Street National Bank of Philadelphia, thereby saving
some $3,000 or $4,000 a year.

Every penny-pinching expedient not only benefited
the syndicate, but swelled Woolworth's personal profit.
His affluence, indeed, was now such that he could
afford to be generous to himself. The yearly trips to
Europe had made him aware of luxury, and he was
reaching for it. He began to assume the clothes and
manners of a merchant prince. However, he was never
a snob. When he turned over the Brooklyn house with
its homely overstuffed furniture to his sister-in-law,
Mary Creighton, and moved the family into a suite in
the fashionable Hotel Savoy on Fifth Avenue, he
explained that the doctor had advised his wife to
leave Brooklyn as she "has had trouble with her
throat."

The Savoy was one of a glittering group of new
palace hotels at the southeast entrance to Central Park.

Like its neighbors, the monumental Plaza and the German renaissance New Netherlands, the Savoy fairly reeked with onyx, marble and other decorative exuberance.

Across the street was the most imposing of all New York's private residences, the huge, ornate chateau of the Cornelius Vanderbilts. Though the Woolworths were not among the Four Hundred invited to Mrs. Vanderbilt's famous white and gold ballroom, this did not faze the five-and-ten magnate in the least. He had no social aspirations.

It was here in the Savoy that the Woolworth's second daughter, Edna, then in her midteens, met young Franklyn Hutton, son of a broker, who was to become her future husband.

In his luxurious new living room Woolworth installed the latest wonder of mechanical music, a player piano; and here he would sit for hours turning rolls, beating silent time to the music, scheming and dreaming. Music still was his great love.

The Christmas trade alone for 1899 totaled almost half a million dollars. Woolworth wrote:

"For the first time in twenty years I spent the night before Christmas at home. It's the last time I'll do so. I'd probably be of little service to any store, yet it is pleasanter to be in the fight at the last moment than to wait at home in suspense."

This Christmas there were no strikes or threatened strikes of the salesgirls. A system of bonuses had been instituted for employees, $5 for each year of service, with a limit of $25.

"Pay this present just before Christmas or the day after," Woolworth cautioned his managers. "Our object is to secure the services of our clerks at a time of the year when competitors are tempting them with higher wages."

Also, since 1896, a week's vacation with pay had been granted all employees of six months' service or longer.

However, continued complaints over the five-and-ten's low wage scale forced Woolworth to establish a minimum rate of $2.50 a week for the girl clerks. In most stores, this minimum was also the maximum.

"If you get hold of a good girl," Woolworth directed, "pay her a little more to keep her from going to some other store. Some of our stores should not pay less than $3 a week. The help can do all window washing and cleaning, even varnishing woodwork. When they work late, don't pay them extra but let them come in later next day."

Each year, when the post-Christmas inventories of all the stores had been sent in, there were days and nights of figuring and checking. Any store whose gross profit was revealed as less than forty per cent would soon be in hot water. But one whose gross profit was too large would find itself in quite as much trouble. The ideal, Woolworth believed, was to be found somewhere between forty and fifty-five per cent. He explained: "It is possible for a store to make more money on 45 to 50 per cent than on 60 per cent and this has been proven . . . when you get 5 cent goods on the 10 cent side . . . it cuts down the sales. The customer finds the same goods in another store."

When a store fell under forty per cent gross, he diagnosed its ailment shrewdly: "First, your clerks or customers are stealing from you. Second, you have too much breakage or waste goods. Third, you are continually pushing goods . . . that pay little profit and letting goods that do pay a big profit sell themselves. Now it is one or all of these three points as you all sell the same goods and pay the same for them . . . any store that can't make forty-five per cent gross profit and twenty per cent net profit is open to ridicule of the whole syndicate."

Woolworth also broke down figures in terms his men could understand. For instance, the total expense to sell $100 worth of goods in one year was $17.52; the following year the cost was $16.68. This left no doubt in anyone's mind but that those costs must go still lower.

In the hiring, coaching and advancement of his men Woolworth displayed judgment akin to genius. "I could always size up a man at a glance," he once boasted. "And no one that I ever fired ever made good anywhere else, so far as I know."

When, in 1898, he bought a group of nine small stores in New England from E. P. Charlton, he placed them in charge of nine young men who had never managed stores before. But all nine were Woolworth-trained from the basement up and hustlers—they made good. One, given charge of a small rundown store in Hartford, Conn., was Byron D. Miller, a former dollar-a-week errand boy. This young man Woolworth, at their first meeting, had picked as a comer.

During this year two more managers, E. C. Webb and C. M. Osborn, were transferred to the New York office and made buyers.

To be tapped for the New York office was the most coveted honor of all. This meant admittance into the Inner Circle and a percentage of the entire syndicate's net profits. Though the exact percentages were matters of strictest secrecy and the contracts subject to yearly revision, these men knew that they had made good and were on the road to wealth.

A list of the buyers in the New York office and goods assigned to each follows:

C. C. Peck: tinware, enameled ware, wire goods,

wooden-ware, twine, wrapping paper, Japanese goods, Fourth of July goods, candy.

C. P. Case: European import goods, domestic crockery, domestic stoneware, domestic yellowware, Easter baskets, tooth brushes, table silver, plated goods, jewelry, rubber toys.

H. A. Moody: European import notions; the following dry goods: towels, wash rags, bibs, handkerchiefs, stamped goods, veilings, laces, Hamburg edgings, ribbons; notions as follows: thread, corset steels, pins, needles, buttons, pocketknives, corset and shoe laces, elastic webs, hose supporters, suspenders, neckwear, lamp wicks, tape measures; leather goods: belts, shawls, straps, pocketbooks, purses; knit goods: ladies' and children's vests, hosiery, mittens, booties.

C. M. Osborn; hardware of all kinds, domestic glassware, whisk brooms, dusters, all brushes except tooth brushes.

B. W. Gage, construction superintendent: everything on the fixture list, including counters, shelving, cash desks, safes, etc.

Besides the managers and buyers, the New York office now employed twenty-three men and women: five typists, seven female bill clerks, nine male book-keepers, one mimeograph operator and one office girl. Lease of two large additional rooms brought the rental to $4,300. Salaries, including that of Hubert Parson, now office manager, were $11,000 a year.

The new century came in booming. In his annual letter Woolworth commented:

I don't remember any year in which there has been such a boom in prices as have come since last July. The first big boom in prices that I remember was in the fall of 1879 when it looked as though the whole five and ten cent business would be shoved right off the face of the earth. It was a hard struggle for me with my limited capital of less than $1,000 but the reaction came in the fore-part of the year 1880 and prices continued to drop for several years. That is the time the five and ten cent business really got a foothold. In 1891 and 1892 there was another boom but the Financial Panic of 1893 struck the country with terrific force and we got another foothold and were able to secure large and fine goods to sell at our prices. 1896 was another panic year and merchandise was slaughtered.

How little did I realize twenty-one years ago when I had that little tumble down store in Lancaster and paid $30 per month rent with a capital of less than $400 that this business would ever grow to such stupendous proportions! And the end has not come yet. Whether the business will grow in the next ten years as it has in the past ten depends upon the energy and ambition of each individual manager as well as myself. Our Capital is $875,000 in stock and fixtures. You are the guardians of this enormous amount of money. I have faith in you and congratulate myself upon having secured such good and capable managers to conduct my business.

We have now at this minute 55 stores running and by the first of July, 1900, we will probably have 58 or more. There seems to be no limit to the number of stores we can open except our capacity to attend to the business. We have on our books many locations. We are limited only in our physical ability to open all these new ventures without getting our fingers burnt.

Woolworth proceeded to open more stores, always on a Saturday, and each opening became a gala event. The formal openings were now preceded on Friday afternoons by a reception and preview inspection to which were invited, as special guests, prominent persons of each neighborhood. A ten-piece orchestra became a feature of these events.

In the new 14th Street store, in New York, opened in June, 1900, and proclaimed "the largest ten-cent store in the world," a pipe organ was installed—to "remain permanently in this store and discourse classical and sentimental music when required." A second Harlem store, at 125th Street and Third Avenue, opened a fortnight later, with a young woman soloist as well as the orchestra.

About this time, young cousin Fred Woolworth became a full-fledged manager and took over the original Harlem store, on 125th Street near Seventh Avenue. He proved to be a young man of ideas, and suggested that he widen the aisles, modernize the front and put in some Frink reflectors to light up window displays. Woolworth told him to go ahead. Sales doubled, and Woolworth promptly did over several other stores, enlarging floor space, rearranging counters, and so on.

At the same time Woolworth moved to give his stores a uniform appearance. Originally he had adopted his red front from the Great Atlantic & Pacific Tea Company, though the gold-leaf gilding of lettering and molding was his own idea. After much experimenting with paints and varnishes, he settled upon a fast and brilliant carmine red for his fronts and show windows. The scraping, sandpapering and painting were all done according to formula. As late as the fall of 1900, some of the smaller stores still had mahogany-colored fronts, but these were brought into conformity with the general scheme as soon as possible.

The most notable event, however, during 1900, was the dedication in November of a five-story and roof garden structure in Lancaster, Pa., in commemoration of the first five-and-ten established there twenty-one years before. It was the first Woolworth Building, and marked the five-and-ten magnate's debut as a landlord. The plot cost $75,000; the building thrice that. The first floor was occupied by a five-and-ten, the four upper floors were rented out as offices.

Every man in the syndicate, from Woolworth down, bent to the task of making the new Lancaster establishment the richest and most imposing store of its type in the world. The result was an unsurpassed display of decorative innovations and iridescent color effects. There were six immense metal show windows, paneled with mirrors, illuminated with incandescent lights, fronting on two streets. The counters were of imitation mahogany and the nine iron columns supporting the ceiling were covered with imitation Siena marble, the work of a group of skilled Italian artisans Woolworth had sent down from New York. In the rear of the store, commanding a view of every part of the floor, was a luxurious office, entered through a plate-glass doorway, guarded by two hand-carved lions. The side walls were done in light green, decorated with gold leaf and laid out in panels with the diamond W trademark emblazoned in gilt and containing the names of all the stores and such slogans as:

The Woolworth stores require and employ five thousand people to sell one hundred million articles annually.

This is the oldest established 5 and 10 cent store in the world.

Goods displayed in the Woolworth stores are collected from all parts of the world.

Nothing in this store over 10 cents.

Large purchases for cash direct from manufacturers explain the high values we offer.

As manager, Woolworth selected a local man, Harry Albright, whom he had met first when Albright was a postman delivering mail to the first Lancaster store. They had struck up a friendship, renewed each time Woolworth visited Lancaster. Finally, Woolworth had offered the postman a job and sent him to Brooklyn and Pittsburgh for training. Now, beaming and happy with his new authority and responsibilities, Manager Albright arranged details for the formal reception and opening. A fourteen-piece orchestra was engaged and masses of cut flowers, palms, ferns and chrysanthemums were artistically arranged throughout the store.

To Woolworth, this opening was as none other. In striped trousers and cutaway, he stepped forward to greet his guests. With him were Mrs. Woolworth and officials of the New York office and their wives. As the orchestra struck up "The Woolworth March," the five-and-ten magnate caught the eye of a reporter who stood near him.

"We've got some of the best people in town here," he whispered delightedly. "Don't it do your heart good?"

In the shimmering magnificence of its latest establishment, the five-and-ten had indeed come of age. Sales for the 59 stores in 1900 passed the $5,000,000 mark.

And the end was not yet in sight.

Chapter IX

The $10,000,000 Corporation

EARLY in 1901 a spare, erect old man, rising eighty, was being shown through the latest addition to Fifth Avenue's Millionaires' Row—a thirty-room mansion at the northeast corner of Eightieth Street. His keen, wind-wrinkled eyes blinked at the red and gilt paneling and wall decorations, the carved and gilded Louis XVI sofas, the gold chairs with tapestry backs in salon and reception rooms, the rich, colorful rugs, the luxurious bedroom suites inlaid in toyon wood. Then he remarked to the stout, beaming gentleman at his side:

"This must have cost a mint of money, Frank."

"A good deal, father, but it's worth it."

"Well, Frank, you always did like to lay it on thick."

Woolworth's father was not the only one who was a bit overwhelmed by the lush magnificence of 990 Fifth Avenue. His wife, Jennie, who grew more retiring with the years, sometimes sighed for the more homely comforts of their earlier dwellings.

To Woolworth, however, the mansion marked a definite milestone in his career. It placed him among the Big Fellows—that florid and flamboyant company of industrial tycoons who'd made their piles in steel, oil, copper and railroads; and who swarmed to New

119

York to splurge. Their ornate mansions, alongside his, also shrieked and reeked of wealth.

The new mansion gave Woolworth the opportunity to indulge to the full his passion for music. In the great drawing room on the second floor, done in carved light oak and gold, he installed an organ that could be played automatically, with a number of ingenious mechanical contrivances worked out by himself.

Behind the ceiling cove colored lights were concealed. The console of the organ was wired so that by pressing a button the room could be thrown into pitch darkness. Another button and a symphony would commence; and throughout the composition the lights would change to follow the music—now amber, then green and then into deep mauve, according to the mood of the piece—all by button control.

Later, by similar means, a fascinating pictorial effect was achieved. Just before the opening of a great orchestral classic, with the room in darkness, a magnificent oil portrait of the composer—Wagner or Beethoven, Liszt or Mendelssohn—would appear in a panel at the top of the wall, at first faintly, then growing clearer and clearer until the vision was enveloped in light. So lifelike was the apparition that the composer himself seemed present, listening to his own music. These portraits, including allegorical backgrounds, were painted for Woolworth by the famous Hungarian artist, Joannes de Tahy.

Finally, sound effects were added. When called for by the music, lightning would flash through the room, thunder would crash and rain descend—behind the walls—in torrents so realistic as to make guests wonder how they were going to get home without a drenching. At the same time even the newels of a new marble stairway and Woolworth's bedposts and clothes closets were piped for sound. When the organ was going at full blast, with sound effects, the whole house seemed to roll and rumble.

Frank Taft, vice president of the Aeolian-Skinner Organ Company, who installed the organ and helped Woolworth work out his mechanical ideas, characterizes the merchant as "a master interpreter with rolls of the world's best music," adding:

"He had hundreds of piano and organ music rolls and several hundred phonograph records. In everything he was a lover of color. Although he did not know a note of music and never played a keyboard or other musical instrument, he had an intuitive musical ear and would have made an outstanding orchestra conductor."

From the new mansion on Millionaires' Row, the Woolworths' eldest daughter, Helena, was married, in the spring of 1904, to Charles E. F. McCann, a likable and brilliant young lawyer. Honor graduate of Fordham University Law School, McCann was a nephew of Richard Croker, the former Tammany boss.

Three years later the second daughter, Edna, was married in the Church of the Heavenly Rest on Fifth Avenue, to Franklyn Laws Hutton, a young stock broker. Hutton, member of a socially prominent family, had formerly lived at the Hotel Savoy.

Another addition to the Woolworth menage during this period was a touring car and a young Franco-Swiss chauffeur named Jules.

It was Carson Peck, his general manager, who first awakened Woolworth's enthusiasm in motoring. Peck had purchased an electric automobile which whizzed along at the amazing speed of twelve miles an hour. Woolworth was impressed at the fast pace of the contraption but he didn't cotton much to the electrics and steamers which then dominated the American motor market. Consequently his first car was a baby-blue Renault, gasoline-propelled, purchased in Paris.

And with the car came the young Franco-Swiss, Jules Billard, one of Renault's crack racing drivers, a Grand Prix winner and expert mechanician. A fancy lured Billard into becoming the millionaire's chauffeur and he remained with Woolworth for many years. They became cronies. A bit of a D'Artagnan, Jules was daring, efficient and hardboiled. Woolworth never questioned his decisions in the "motor department."

Each January, Woolworth and his chief detail man, Bookkeeper Parson, locked themselves in a room at the new Fifth Avenue mansion and slaved over the yearly inventories. It was a torturous tussle. Promptly on February 1, each manager received a check for his share of the previous year's profits plus a detailed letter of criticism and suggestion, both signed by Woolworth.

The files and letters spell the story of the Woolworth Syndicate's progress:

Seven small stores were opened in 1902 and a similar number in 1903. Among the latter was a mammoth establishment on Market Street, Philadelphia. Other stores were improved and enlarged. The syndicate totaled 76 stores. Goods were now purchased far in advance and stored for shipment in warehouses in Newark and New York.

Figures for 1902 showed the extent and variety of the merchandise:

Of $5,050,000 worth of goods purchased, some twenty per cent, or $1,048,000, was bought abroad. Amounts spent for leading domestic items were: candy, $672,000; jewelry, $253,000; stationery and novels, $326,000; ribbons, $168,000; hosiery and knit goods, $129,000; notions and novelties, $404,000; hardware, $264,000; tinware and enameled ware, $255,000; glassware, $245,000; crockery, $210,000; toys and games, $198,000. The leading foreign items were: Japanese goods, $72,951; laces and Hamburgs, $129,788; notions and novelties, $157,000; china, $248,737; crockery, $74,866; dolls, $65,533; toys and games, $121,301; tree ornaments, $65,525.

Paying spot cash, the Woolworth buyers underbid all competitors in Europe. This resulted in constant discussion with the government over the classification of goods and the amount of duty due.

"The government is continually raising our invoices," complained Woolworth, "and claiming we are not paying enough duty on our import goods. Our buyers purchase cheaply in Europe and the government claims we do not pay the market price. Mr. Parson and Mr. Case, also Mr. Moody, are kept busy attending appraisers' hearings and settling these disputes and differences."

In 1902, wage scales—another continuous and chronic cause of conflict—were boosted to a minimum of $3 a week. As a further concession it was decreed that for the third week before Christmas all salespeople, old and new, were to receive 75 cents a day, 85 cents for the second week, and the unprecedented amount of $1 a day during the strainful week before Christmas.

Emphasizing the importance of the $3-a-week wage to storekeepers who were tempted to pay less, Woolworth warned:

"We must pay enough to keep the department stores from taking away our best salesladies. I would like to increase salaries but at present don't want to put down an ironclad rule other than the $3 a week minimum. That you must pay and I don't want to find any girls under fifteen, especially those in short dresses, working in our stores."

And to insure the undivided attention of managers and executives, a clause was inserted prominently in every contract, reading:

I agree during the term of this contract not to be interested in any other store or any other business, directly or indirectly, that will occupy my time during business hours, and I agree not to speculate in stocks, grain or securities or enter into any game of chance.

Previously (in 1897) Woolworth had felt obliged to warn his men against speculation with this confession:

August 26, 1897.

About 12 years ago I had a little experience of speculating in stocks myself, although I have never been guilty of buying stocks on the margin. I was running the little store in Lancaster, Pa., and I had some spare money which I wanted to invest . . . so I commenced by buying a few railroad stocks, and before I was aware of it I was paying much more attention to the quotations in the Stock Market than I was to running the store, and in three months I was losing my trade, and I decided then and there to let stocks alone and to attend to business . . . Now, if any managers have spare money they would like to invest, I advise them to put it into bonds or mortgages or something that does not fluctuate very much.

Again and again, Woolworth instructed his store managers in their attitude toward their customers:

One manager writes in about my demand for increased sales: "Do you want me to go on the street and pull 'em in?" No, you don't have to bark for customers. That method is too ancient for us. But you can pull customers into your stores and they won't know it. Draw them in with attractive window displays and when you get them in have a plentiful showing of the window goods on the counters.

Make it a rule not to bore or annoy customers. Let them look around to their heart's content. Don't try and press goods on them. The most successful merchants in the United States, John Wanamaker and Marshall Field, will not allow a clerk to approach a customer. They make their stores Fairs and a person can go entirely through them without once being pressed to buy anything. Make your customers feel at home. Have waiting rooms and rest rooms. Encourage people to meet their friends in your store. Give them something free. I was in a store the other day where they furnished free ice water and it made a hit. The same store set up a pair of Fairbanks scales with a sign: "See how much you weigh? Free." Both are good ideas for us.

Special sales are fine if the bargains are real. Be sure your ten cent specials cannot be bought anywhere else for less than 20 or 25 cents. Remember our advertisements are in our show windows and on our counters.

To impress upon the managers the importance of giving the customers what they wanted, Woolworth selected a concrete example:

We have found on investigation that the average customer prefers the small 6 inch nickel shears to the larger ones. Yet inspection shows

that only two or three out of thirty or forty
stores keep in stock the smaller shears, which give
us much greater profits than the larger ones. This
is only one item in our multitudinous line of
goods, yet it shows you have been buying things
the customer does not want.

Carson Peck had taken candy under his wing and
built it into the syndicate's most lucrative department.

"No retail concern in this little world of ours," he
reported, "sells as much candy as the combined Woolworth stores. No manager should be satisfied unless
he makes his candy sales pay his rent."

Incidentally, the conscientious Peck liberally sam-
pled each new variety of candy offered, thus inno-
cently inviting a condition which was to cost him his
life.

There was a tenderness, a humanness, a scrupulous
sense of fairness about Carson Peck that made the
general manager the most loved, certainly the most
respected, man in the organization. He particularly
championed the ambitious young men who were training (beginning inevitably in the basement) for future
store management. Peck took some managers to task
because they did not "appreciate the value" of these
assistants.

"These young men are anxious to be of service," he
wrote, "and they should have a reasonable amount of
instruction in business methods. Don't think you are
getting the best service out of a young man by simply
showing him how quickly he can get a crate of
crockery in the cellar unpacked and stored away. He
wants to realize how necessary it is . . . to turn the
contents of cask into money with a little profit for the
benefit of the concern. He wants to know why it is
necessary to be so careful in watching freight bills,

watching count, watching the quality of the goods received and reporting whether he considers them good . . . When he is moved from the basement to the store floor he wants to be a little more than the ordinary floor walker, he wants to be instilled with . . . the purpose of the business which is to make money and it does not hurt . . . to show . . . how more profit can be made if it is shown up in this way or that way. I am speaking more particularly for those who are considering the possibility of becoming candidates some day for manager. This is simply a plea for you to treat them right . . . Don't think you can squeeze the life out of him and that he will stand it gracefully . . . I just learned today of a young man sent to one of the stores as a six dollar man about six or eight months ago . . . and is still a six dollar man today. I would like to ask you what kind of enthusiasm that man can be expected to put into his work. How can you expect him to come one half an hour earlier in the morning and stay until 10 or 11 o'clock at night when . . . he . . . has to fill up on mush and milk for dinner or put up at the cheapest boarding house . . . If he gets to be worth $15 a week don't feel you are in duty bound to hold him down."

This letter revealed a condition about which Woolworth professed, a few days later, to be shocked. He told the store managers that these young men, if they were any good at all, certainly were worth more than $6 a week. Their salaries, he said, should be increased each month, from $6 to $7 to $8 to $9 to $10. After five months a manager could use his discretion in regard to further advances, but the New York office, he said, wanted to receive information as to their progress. Worthy candidates for store manager were to be told it was their duty to get in touch with headquarters. The "learners" were the cadets of the busi-

ness, and Woolworth's immediate plans called for the
training of future officers at accelerated pace.

After a comparatively dull period, so far as expansion
was concerned, Woolworth in 1904 took a decided
plunge into new territory—the West.

Previously, when asked about the possibility of
opening stores in that section of the country, he'd
replied: "No, we'll fill up the East first." The chief
deterrent, however, had been the high cost of freight-
age to points so far from New York. This drawback
was now ironed out by "persuading" Eastern manufacturers, under promise of larger orders, to bear the
increased shipping charges.

Early on the morning of February 19, 1904, without telling a soul, Woolworth and C. C. Griswold
slipped off on a train for the West; and, within a
fortnight, Woolworth had inspected, bought and paid
for twenty-one stores—all operated by independent
five-and-ten men, all on paying basis. The list follows:

From Pfohl & Smith:

Minneapolis, Minn.	Marshalltown, Iowa	Joplin, Mo.
La Crosse, Wis.	Fargo, N. D.	Denver, Colo.
Des Moines, Iowa	St. Paul, Minn.	Pueblo, Colo.
Sioux City, Iowa	Springfield, Ill.	Lincoln, Neb.
Cedar Rapids, Iowa	St. Joseph, Mo.	

From S. D. Rider:

South Bend, Ind.	Davenport, Iowa	Lafayette, Ind.

From George B. Carey:

Joliet, Ill.	Dubuque, Iowa	Aurora, Ill.

From John W. Carey:

Decatur, Ill.

This invasion of the West was one of Woolworth's boldest strokes. He had determined upon it suddenly when he learned through trade channels that Pfohl & Smith might consider an offer for their chain.

To handle the new units, a Western office was opened in the Railway Exchange Building in Chicago. Griswold was placed in charge, with H. W. Cowan and Lambert G. Smith, formerly of Pfohl & Smith, as assistants. Woolworth's keen instinct for executive talent led him also to select L. J. Surdam, manager of the store in Minneapolis, as his Western inspector.

To these men, Woolworth gave contracts providing for participation in the profits of all the stores, new and old, explaining:

"I want my executives interested in every store we own. The prosperity of one is the prosperity of all. Unless we had worked together as a system, we could not possibly have secured the great advantage of equal freight rates for the western stores. Mr. Griswold has been given authority to deal with certain western manufacturers but the vast bulk of the buying will continue to be done in New York. New York will always remain general headquarters."

Three other managers were promoted to the New York executive force—C. B. Winslow of Worcester, George W. Strongman of Washington, and Frank B. Carpenter of Philadelphia.

The following August, Woolworth bought twelve stores operated by one Murphy in and near McKeesport, Pa; and four stores run by independents in Massachusetts. Thus thirty-seven stores were purchased and paid for outright in 1904. In addition, the Western chain was enlarged by new units in Topeka, Kansas, and Springfield, Ohio; and in the East five new Woolworths made their bow.

In all, during 1904, a total of forty-four stores were added to the seventy-six already operating—making a grand total of 120 under the Woolworth banner. It was by far the greatest plunge Woolworth had made in any one year.

And it hastened a move now recognized as inevitable: the business must incorporate.

Five-and-ten could no longer remain a one-man show, its prosperity and that of thousands dependent upon the health and continued activity of a single individual. The risk had been sharply borne in upon Woolworth two years before when a nervous attack sent him to bed for three weeks. Ever since he had worried over the fate of the business if anything should happen to him.

Gradually and reluctantly he came to realize that if the enterprise were to be perpetuated, he must form a corporation.

Accordingly, one morning the five-and-ten men received the momentous news that hereafter the business would be conducted through a $10,000,000 stock corporation.

"This will be the last letter I shall ever write to you as individual owner and proprietor of all the five-and-ten-cent stores running January 1, 1905," Woolworth informed his managers. "It is a sad occasion and I will tell you later on why I am transferring my business to a corporation. Hereafter I will write to you as a representative of a corporation. I am sorrowful but modern methods must be pursued. Twenty-six years I have endeavored to conduct five-and-ten-cent stores on an honorable and systematic and paying basis. But time is fast flying away and I cannot expect always to be in control of this vast property."

The corporation—organized under the laws of the State of New York and retaining the name F. W. Woolworth & Company—came into being February 16, 1905. There were 50,000 shares of preferred and 50,000 shares of common stock, each with par value of $100. The preferred stock was to draw 7% dividends, payable quarterly on April 1, July 1, October 1 and January 1. The common stock guaranteed no fixed return but its owners held all powers of control provided the preferred dividends were met.

The common stock—which eventually was to yield fabulous returns—was parceled out, at Woolworth's discretion, among himself and executives of the New York and Chicago offices. The preferred stock was offered at par to the store managers and other employees. There was no public subscription. Thus five-and-ten remained strictly a family affair.

The organization meeting elected Woolworth, C. C. Peck, C. P. Case, H. A. Moody and H. T. Parson directors; and these elected the following officers: Woolworth, president; Peck and Case, vice presidents; Parson, secretary and treasurer; C. C. Griswold and H. W. Cowan, assistant treasurers. These men and the following executives signed agreements pledging themselves to remain with the corporation until January 1, 1910: B. W. Gage, C. M. Osborn, J. H. Strongman, A. E. Ivie, Walter Williams, C. S. Winslow, George W. Strongman, Lambert G. Smith, L. J. Surdam, Frank B. Carpenter.

In an intimate letter to his men, Woolworth explained that formation of the corporation was the only way to protect the business and to insure its permanency.

"The ties that have bound us together so long are not broken," he wrote. "We are now more united than ever. Now every manager of every store, every clerk and office boy, every saleslady is safe because no matter what happens to me or to any officer of the company the business goes on just the same. Before you were all taking chances in betting on my health and ability. Every time I have been sick or unable to work I have thought of the terrible responsibilities resting on my shoulders and of so many people depending on my health. The corporation is more expensive than the old way of doing business but that is the penalty for security.

"We could have capitalized for much more and sold stock to the public," he added, "but we're not going to do that. Subscriptions have already been received for 6,431 preferred shares. I am not anxious to dispose of any stock for as fast as I sell my income is reduced and I think I'll put a price of $110 a share on it after the first dividend is declared. However, if any manager wants a little more, I may be able to accommodate him at par, even after April 1. Now about the security. Is this stock worth $100 a share? Is the business worth $5,000,000? All I can say is I was offered that much for it before it was ever turned into a corporation. Preferred stockholders really have the first mortgage on the entire property, though power of control is vested in the common stock. The common stock is held by myself and the managers of the New York and Chicago offices only and none of this stock is for sale at present."

Self-interest Woolworth recognized as the most potent spur in human endeavor and, as time went on, he used his ownership of majority stock in the corporation to stimulate this instinct. Each new manager was permitted to acquire, on liberal terms, a small block of the 7% preferred stock. The controlling common stock Woolworth guarded as though it were the Holy Grail, releasing it only to the small inner circle of executives whose cooperation he considered essential in running the organization. However, the men below,

even the $6-a-week "learners" in the basements, knew
that they would be cut in on the Big Melon when and
if they were admitted to the inner circle.

As befitting a $10,000,000 corporation, the five-and-
ten in 1905 moved into opulent new offices in the
Stewart Building. In comparison with the drab old
quarters, the new offices, overlooking City Hall Park,
shone like Joseph's coat. There were an imposing
entrance hall, sample room and private offices for the
leading executives. There were overhead lighting and
mahogany furniture, upholstered couches and gaily
painted wainscoting.

Woolworth now sat at a great desk of mahogany
and gold. His office was a chromatic joy: its three
windows, opening on the park, curtained in green
velour; the parquet floor of teakwood covered with a
rich rug of warm golden brown; the walls paneled;
the chair of mahogany and gold upholstered in green
morocco.

"This may seem wasteful to some of you," Woolworth wrote the boys, "but you have no idea the impression our fine new office makes on visitors. Now
they realize they are in the presence of a successful
and important concern. Why, even landlords are impressed with our magnificence and system! The five
and ten cent business is no longer a Cheap John affair.
We cater to the masses but we have gained the respect and the trade also of the medium and wealthy
classes. Only the other night, at the banquet of the
Lancaster, Pa., Board of Trade, I found that almost
all the articles on the table had been purchased at our
Lancaster store. We ought to feel proud."

The five-and-ten was indeed on the commercial
map. The new offices were crowded continually with
manufacturers and salesmen soliciting orders—now

as eager as they had once been aloof. New gadgets
and toys and household devices were exhibited in
every free corner. A Woolworth o.k. on any one of
them might mean a fortune. Then there were landlords leases, real estate men boosting new locations,
freight and steamship agents and, last but not least,
bankers and representatives of banks offering themselves as custodians of those enticing pyramids of
nickels and dimes.

Woolworth manufactured not a single item of the
thousands on his list and never intended to. His buyers,
however, now went direct to the factories. The manufacturers not only welcomed their orders but in many
cases rebated to Woolworth commissions which formerly had gone to jobbers, salesmen and other middlemen. It was a mutually satisfactory and lucrative
alliance.

One of Woolworth's methods of insuring lower
prices was to stir up rivalries not only among the
manufacturers but among his own buyers. He was a
perfect genius at this and made a game of it. He invited confidential complaints and communications and,
when he got two men roaring angrily at each other,
would chuckle gleefully and remark:

"Now I've got you. You are losing your tempers and
now maybe we'll get to the bottom of this business."

New men were climbing the Woolworth ladder.
Harry Albright, the ex-postman, and Byron Miller, the
former dollar-a-week errand boy, became inspectors
for the Eastern stores; William J. Rand, Jr., inspector
in the West.

The march of dimes went forward at double quick.
In 1906 sales fell just short of $15,000,000 and the
number of stores grew to 160.

The new atmosphere of luxury did not distract
Woolworth's attention from details. These he watched

with his usual hawklike prescience. He was pleased to learn that presses for baling straw and waste paper, which had been placed in most of the stores, were rapidly paying for themselves. Instead of paying cartmen to get rid of rubbish, the waste paper and straw fetched from ten to thirty cents a bundle. The boys called this the "velvet department." Within a short time it was swelling profits to the tune of $1,000 a week. The boss was not so pleased over other items, raising hob because it cost 67 cents in wrapping paper and twine to sell $100 worth of goods, as against 59 cents the previous year.

Again the stores were warned not to sacrifice sales volume for the promise of bigger profits on individual items:

> Some envelopes were furnished you to sell at two packages for five cents. At this rate they show a good big profit. But there is so little difference between the two for five and the five cent envelopes that many managers were tempted to put the two for fives on the five cent counter. Now what sort of way is that to do business when you can go into any drug store or stationery store and get good envelopes at five cents a package? The same criticism goes for those of you who are trying to sell for ten cents goods that should be sold at five.

Meanwhile, new stores were continually being opened. Behind one of them lies a story.

In 1879, when Woolworth was struggling to keep his pioneer Lancaster venture alive, he was aided by the prosperous Philadelphia importing firm of Conway Brothers. This house had sold toys and dolls to him direct rather than through jobbers, and befriended him in other ways. Afterward the brothers Conway went into the retail variety business and Woolworth lost track of them. One day, twenty-six years later, while on a store-hunting scout, he entered a dilapidated establishment in Camden, New Jersey, and heard a clerk address an elderly, faded woman as "Mrs. Conway." She proved to be the widow of one of the brothers. The store, with its pitiful stock, represented the remnants of her worldly possessions. Woolworth's eyes filled with tears, he told her of her husband's kindness to him and bought the store at a liberal valuation set by himself.

By the spring of 1908, the stores totaled 189; their administration was becoming unwieldy, even for a man of Woolworth's genius at detail.

Accordingly, it was decided to divide the stores into geographical groups and to place a responsible official in charge of each. Six districts were created, each in command of a superintendent. The superintendents were former inspectors. Each was assigned headquarters in the leading city of his division and given direct responsibility for the conduct and progress of all stores in the district. The list, together with territory covered:

District No. 1; headquarters Boston; Superintendent, B. D. Miller; 37 stores located in Maine, New Hampshire, Massachusetts and Rhode Island.

District No. 2; Albany; F. B. Carpenter; 35 stores in Connecticut, Vermont and New York state down to the Harlem River.

District No. 3; New York City; H. H. Albright; 28 stores in Long Island, New Jersey, and the city of New York below the Harlem River.

District No. 4; Philadelphia; E. Z. Nutting; 39 stores in Pennsylvania, Delaware, Maryland, District of Columbia, Virginia and West Virginia.

District No. 5; Chicago; L. J. Surdam; 29 stores in Ohio, Indiana, Illinois, Michigàn, Wisconsin, Minnesota, North Dakota, South Dakota.

District No. 6; Omaha; W. J. Rand, Jr.; 21 stores in Iowa, Missouri, Nebraska, Kansas, Colorado, Wyoming, Utah.

This regional system, expanded and developed, became the five-and-ten's permanent form of organization.

In the course of eight years, despite the short and dramatic panic of 1907, Woolworth had tripled his stores and quadrupled his sales. The latter were now over the $20,000,000 mark.

Pleased with himself and the world in general, the portly Peter Pan of the red fronts observed to his boys:

"Did it ever occur to you that our business is an indirect charity and of benefit to the people at large? While we are in business for profit, we are also the means of making thousands of people happy. The more stores we create the more good we do humanity."

Indeed, as Woolworth sat at his gold and mahogany desk and gazed beyond the green velour curtains framing his office windows, the horizons seemed illimitable for his five-and-ten.

Chapter X

England Growls but Goes
Five-and-Ten

THE year 1909 found the Woolworth corporation firmly established and of increasing importance in the American business world. Its ornate offices were alive with activity and evidences of prosperity. Manufacturers now came a-courting in droves, vying to produce the most enticing bargains for the five-and-ten-cent counters.

The key executives at headquarters, those men who had stuck to Woolworth through the long grind, were now patting themselves on the back. As members of the inner New York circle, participating in the profits, they had already acquired neat little nest eggs—and could vision for the future wealth beyond their wildest expectations. Life, indeed, seemed fair.

Into the midst of this period of complacency, Woolworth dropped a bombshell. He proposed to open a chain of stores in England.

The response, or rather lack of response, would have dampened the ardor of anyone except the corpulent, keen blue-eyed headman of the five-and-ten.

His lieutenants—Peck, Case, Parson, Ivie, Moody and the rest—were stunned, and not a little frightened.

138

They suspected that Woolworth, who was now nearing fifty-seven, had reached that delicate time of life
when judgment sometimes goes haywire. To a man,
they chorused disapproval. Why tackle a foreign market when so much remained to be done in the U.S.A.?
Why risk the unknown when they had gotten so
beautifully organized in territory that was familiar?
The British were slow and stolid, and only a miracle
could make them change their buying habits. Et cetera,
et cetera.

Woolworth, however, brushed the objections aside.
Behind his seemingly adventitious decision lay many
years of thought and observation, beginning back in
1890 on his first stroll along London streets when he
wrote: "I think a good penny and six pence store run
by a live Yankee would create a sensation here, but
perhaps not." In the years intervening he had often
dreamed of invading Great Britain and, on his numerous visits abroad, had pored over maps and noted the
density of population in certain areas. In his mind's
eye he saw millions of potential customers in England.

Now, in 1909, instinct told him the time was ripe
for the British adventure. He called for volunteers.

None of the veteran executives responded. But three
of the younger men did. With two of these we are
acquainted: Fred Woolworth, his cousin, now manager of the Sixth Avenue store; and Byron D. Miller,
the former errand boy, now a superintendent. The
third was Samuel H. Balfour, manager of the 14th
Street store and of the reshipping warehouse attached
thereto.

Balfour, who was somewhat older than the others,
had entered Woolworth's service under rather unusual circumstances.

Back in the '80's Balfour was bookkeeper for a drygoods house in Ogdensburg, New York, which held

a patent on a so-called popgun and peashooter arrangement for carrying cash in a little box on a wire to the cashier's desk. When this firm learned that Woolworth had installed a similar device in his small Lancaster store, it had Balfour write to him. Several letters were exchanged and Woolworth was struck with the bookkeeper's beautiful handwriting—accomplished, incidentally, with his left hand. Years passed and then the two met accidentally in Watertown, which was also Balfour's native town. Woolworth hired him and the modest and able Balfour thereafter advanced steadily, becoming a valued merchandising expert for the five-and-ten. Woolworth was pleased when this particular protégé enlisted for the British adventure.

Balfour's health later failed and he returned to America to meet tragic death in a fire. Save for these twists of fate, he would have shared the swelling wealth that came to Fred Woolworth and Byron Miller for their pioneering part in the British project.

"I don't know to this day why I enlisted," grins the gray-haired Miller, a retired Woolworth veteran who divides his time between beautiful homes in Falmouth, Maine, and Palm Beach, Florida. "All the big men in the office, Peck, Case and the others, solemnly warned me against taking a chance. But I was young and brash and the Chief had the most blandishing ways of any man I ever knew."

The Argonauts sailed on Decoration Day, 1909. In the party were F. W. Woolworth and wife and their youngest daughter, Jessie; Mr. and Mrs. Fred Woolworth; Mr. and Mrs. Balfour and their young daughter; and Miller.

Establishing headquarters in London, the four men began surveying the field. The British masses, they found, were served by so-called "Penny Bazaars," most of which were simply sidewalk stalls offering a very limited variety of goods, displayed generally in baskets. Woolworth quickly concluded that he could crush such opposition with a chain of bright, commodious, well-stocked red fronts modeled upon his American establishments. He decided to call them three-and-six-pence stores, 3d. and 6d. being the nearest equivalent in British currency to five cents and ten cents.

When the search for store locations began, Woolworth and his companions traveled quietly by train and for a time succeeded to keeping their mission a secret.

Hitherto Woolworth had visited England only as a customer and his experiences had been exceedingly pleasant. Now, however, when he came to subtract from, instead of fatten, the British pocketbook, he found both his reception and conditions vastly different. Americans were generally looked upon (often with reason) as vulgarians and sharpers. The only American merchant who'd sought to break into the retail drygoods trade was Selfridge, and his expensive emporium on Oxford Street was going none too well.

Woolworth's first letter home describes some of the path-finders' travails:

We have visited Northampton, Southampton, Portsmouth, Croyden, Brighton, Reading, Hammersmith, Kensington, Birmingham, Wolverhampton, Coventry, Liverpool and Manchester, all of which we consider good locations for our business. But stores here are too small and shallow. A store will have a fine front and show windows 25 to 50 feet wide, yet is only 50 to 75 feet deep. The reason is that customers do most of their shopping from the show windows. You will find the sidewalks crowded with people looking in the windows and expect to see the store full. But go inside and you will notice only one or two cutomers. The moment you go in you are expected to buy and to have made your choice from the window. They give you an icy stare if you follow the American custom of just going in to look around. Even the famous Harrods of London is only 150 feet deep by 300 frontage.

Selfridge's is the only department store that looks like an American establishment. His building is five stories high with a fine roof tea garden. He is a former partner of Marshall Field of Chicago and has spent an enormous amount of money and may make a success in time. He has been trying to float some stock in his corporation but without much success. Most Englishmen think he will fail. There seems to be a prejudice against him, in fact against all foreigners invading this territory. Americans in many lines of business have given up, especially manufacturers who have been trying to open a market here for American goods. Most goods here are better made and cheaper than in America. A better show case can be bought here for $200 than in New York for $550. Goods which we sell for ten cents are six to eight cents here. Five cent goods can be bought for two or three cents. This means that when we open in England we shall sell very few American goods.

We have no walkover here. British business men are as bright, alert and smart as the average American. Some of their ideas we would do well to copy. This trip has been a great education. We have simply been studying conditions so as not to make any more mistakes than we can help.

Yet we intend to take the plunge and open a few stores. We have already made an offer for a location in a large city. How much business we shall do only time can tell.

Sundays we drive in the country in our automobile. It is not safe to drive fast because of crooked roads and high hedges. Bicycles are a great annoyance. They are used as extensively as in the old days, 15 or 20 years ago, in America. We are on the railroads nearly every day. Trains and service are better than ours. Trains go 70 to 75 miles an hour and are seldom a minute late. You give up your ticket at the station you get off at and one is not bothered with conductors, porters and baggage men and newsboys.

Their mission, however, could not be kept secret for long. Soon trade journals and even the London press took notice of it. The *Draper's Journal* and other trade publications waxed sarcastic and predicted failure; while the great *Daily Mail,* in an editorial blast on the "American invasion," compared Woolworth to Barnum and warned the British public against his cheap, shoddy bazaars. Woolworth took the criticism in good part.

"I remember one day we were lunching in the Strand," recalls Mr. Miller, "and fell into conversation with a man from the States, manager of one of the early American motion picture houses. He made a scraping gesture with his thumb and forefinger and said he was in England for just one purpose, to get all he could out of the 'limeys,' and supposed we were there for the same reason. Woolworth denounced such an attitude as wrong and pointed out to us that this type of American was largely responsible for creating the prejudice we found ourselves facing. This prejudice was so strong that we sometimes met personal abuse."

To neutralize this antipathy, Woolworth decided to add an Englishman to his group. Through Edward Owen of Birmingham, buyer for Wanamaker and other large American stores, he came upon a bright, energetic young man named William L. Stephenson. Stephenson, who had been Owen's assistant, was a fountain of enterprise, humor and ability. Today he is chairman of British Woolworth and entertains royalty upon his yacht.

Meanwhile, the F. W. Woolworth & Company, Ltd., was formed with a capital of £50,250. There were 5,000 shares of preference (preferred) stock at ten pounds per share and 5,000 shares of ordinary (common) stock at one shilling per share. Two-fifths of the capitalization, Woolworth reported, "is already put up in cash." To his skeptical viceroys in New York he wrote:

> Our offer for a store has been practically accepted but papers have not been signed yet. We find it no small undertaking to start our business in England. My opinion of the average Englishman being rather slow was an error. We may get done up yet. What astonishes us most is the low price merchandise of all kinds is sold at; and in some cases the very low per cent of profit. We have been learning some new trick every day and are absorbing all the information we can get before we put up any money.
>
> Within a radius of 20 miles from the city of Manchester, I am told there are 9,500,000 souls, more people than in any other district of the same area on the globe, not even excepting the congested areas of China. The whole section is

composed of industries that have made England the manufacturing center of the world. The principal industry is the manufacture of cotton goods. Yet Manchester City does not look as lively and up to date to us as Liverpool, 35 miles away, which has only 700,000 to 800,000 people.

My time is taken up trying to get this infant of English stores started so that she can walk alone. When that happens she must be watched every day until she is finally able to take care of herself. At times the difficulties we have encountered have seemed insurmountable. However, pluck and perseverance have overcome all obstacles thus far. The buying power of the New York office is a great help now in securing low prices for goods we need.

The activities of the five-and-ten men were noted with curiosity and ill-concealed hostility by their neighbors. One rival merchant remarked grimly:

"The Americans are opening in Liverpool to be near the boat for 'ome."

But nothing daunted Woolworth.

"I really begin to enjoy the gloomy predictions of failure," he observed. "They remind me so much of what I used to be told so often in America. Our lease was signed Friday, August 13, the government signed our incorporation papers July 23, 'skidoo day,' but we are not superstitious. I predict a moderate success here at first and eventually a big assured success."

Leaving his men to handle the details, Woolworth took a brief holiday trip to Switzerland with his wife and daughter. They found the National Hotel in Lucerne, where they stopped, overrun with matrimonially inclined counts, barons, princes and dukes, and Woolworth commented, feelingly:

"These cheap titled people are after the American girl and her money. You must respect their good judgment in hoping to get both money and a fine-looking wife. But the poor American father and mother over here have their troubles if they are not sympathetic with this sort of courtship."

He touched the same theme in more postive terms a month later when motoring through the English countryside and visiting Blenheim Castle, near Oxford.

The Castle is the home of the Duke of Marlborough and *was* the home of the Duchess (Consuela Vanderbilt) who now refuses to live with him. The famous estate of 70,000 acres is sadly run down because the Duke is no longer in receipt of enormous sums from his American father-in-law, W. K. Vanderbilt. The Duke spends all he can get hold of in fast living in Paris, London, Monte Carlo, etc. He has not the power to sell his land or great works of art, sculpture or furniture. How much better it would have been for him if he had been obliged to learn the five and ten cent business at $6 per week and become a commercial man instead of as we see him now— no use to anyone and no satisfaction to himself.

The bright and shining Liverpool store opened with a band concert Friday afternoon, November 5, 1909, and for business the following morning. During the two days 60,000 people passed through its portals, but the majority were drawn by curiosity and the sales were slow by American standards. B. D. Miller remembers some of his first visitors holding up American bathroom and kitchen gadgets and asking in wonderment:

"I say, wot's this blawsted thing for? Wotta you do with it?"

Nevertheless, American glassware, candy and other goods sold freely, as did British pottery, enamelware, etc.; and, within a very short time, sales improved and steadied.

Woolworth missed the opening. He had been called back to New York. Chaffing at his desk, chewing his cigar nervously, he studied the daily cables from Liverpool. Finally he could stand the suspense no longer, and booked passage for England. Sailing with him was E. J. Smith of Buffalo, one of his best store scouters. Now while the iron was hot was the time, he felt, to strike out for more British business.

"The store is simply beautiful, the handsomest in Liverpool," he wrote upon arrival. "Its wonders have reached London and all the other cities of England. Our chief competitor, who has one hundred and thirty 6½d. bazaars all over England is rumored ready to give up and not fight us. How can he when he confines himself to one price in his small stores and only carries china, glass and enamelware while we carry 1d., 3d., and 6d. goods and our lines are unlimited? His store in a poor location in Liverpool has cut prices to 4½d. but does not affect our trade. We are going to look for more stores and sail on the *Mauretania* December 11."

Woolworth and his Buffalo expert proceeded to lease five more store locations in England. A second Liverpool establishment, in London Road, was obtained from Owen Owen, a department store owner, who told Woolworth he'd no idea "the bazaar business could be elevated to such a high standard." Store No. 3 was in Preston, a coast city of some 111,000 population north of Liverpool. Properties were obtained also in Manchester, Leeds and Hull.

There was still prejudice, however, and many refused to have their properties "disgraced by any cheap American bazaar." One landlord turned Woolworth down after sending his brother to look over the Liverpool store. The brother reported that the store sold, among other articles, tomahawks (hatchets) and the fair and enlightened people of England never would put up with such uncivilized instruments of torture.

"Many of the English," Woolworth observed, "do not like private limited companies, which have sometimes cheated them. However, we have worked hard and spent a lot of money and we are going to win. We will have six stores in operation by July 1, 1910."

Returning to one of the most satisfactory Christmases in years, even the irrepressible Shaman of the five-and-tens could not foresee that he had launched an enterprise which eventually was to become actually more lucrative than his vast American chain of stores. For the five-and-ten (really the six-and-twelve) caught on in England more rapidly than it had in America.

By 1912, there were twenty-eight stores, all but two managed by Englishmen, and the year's net profits were well over $100,000. Carson Peck shook his head and remarked: "The little baby we have over in England has gotten out of swaddling clothes." Case, Moody and the rest had to admit their chief had accomplished the impossible.

So deeply did the three-and-sixes wedge their way into British life that many English people, coming to America for the first time, would note the familiar red front and exclaim:

"Oh, you have Woolworths in the United States, also!"

Chapter XI

The $65,000,000 Merger

MEANWHILE, in America, Woolworth had rivals; some friendly, some not so friendly.

Among his allies were Seymour Knox, his cousin and early partner, Fred M. Kirby, Earle Charlton and, of course, his brother, C. S. Woolworth. Three of these names are familiar to us. The fourth, Charlton, had been drawn into the five-and-ten-cent business through Knox.

Earle Perry Charlton, a tall, humorful young man, who hailed originally from Chester, Connecticut, had been crack traveling salesman for the Boston firm of Thomas C. Newell & Company, specializing in household necessities. On one of his periodical road trips, he remarked one day to his customer, Knox:

"There is a great opportunity for your business in the New England states."

"Why don't you try it with me?" was the answer, and the firm of Knox & Charlton was born. Their first venture, in the spring of 1890, was in Fall River, Massachusetts. This was followed by stores under the Knox & Charlton name in Hartford and New Britain, Conn., and in Lowell, Mass. Later, Charlton branched out as head of a flourishing organization of his own and introduced the five-and-ten to Canada and the Pacific Coast.

From the beginning each of these men—increasing the number of his stores slowly in comparison with the bolder rush of Frank Woolworth—worked in closest association with him. As far back as March, 1892, when Knox and Charlton were still partners, this significant entry appeared in Frank Woolworth's ledger:

> We have been trying to make a deal with the United States Glass Company since January 1 and have at last succeeded in making a deal whereby we will be entitled to a rebate on January 1, 1893 according to our purchases. And in order to make the purchases as large as possible we have induced S. H. Knox, F. M. Kirby and C. S. Woolworth to help us out on quantities. All goods they purchase for their stores will be counted with our stores as one firm and give us rebate according to the total purchases of about 35 stores. If our purchases reach $25,000 for the year we will all get a rebate of 7%. But this 7% is the maximum of rebate.

This arrangement was followed by many others. One was an unwritten (never violated) pledge not to invade one another's territory. This, together with the pooling of purchases and free exchange of information, gave them a tremendous competitive advantage. Hence, by the early 1900's, Knox, Kirby, Charlton and C. S. Woolworth each individually owned neat and growing chains of five-and-tens. Their stores, in fact, totaled altogether almost as many as those operated by Frank Woolworth.

With these "rivals," together with his old boss, W. H. Moore, who still conducted the Watertown emporium, Woolworth was on the friendliest terms. Indeed,

they were as the fingers of a hand. They continued
to buy goods together in large quantities, to exchange
trade secrets, and with their families visited in one
another's homes. Scarcely a year passed that one or
another of them didn't go to Europe with Woolworth
or join him at Palm Beach. Each of these men, Knox
and Kirby in particular, were rapidly becoming powers
in their own bailiwicks and, as their stores and incomes
grew, developed a keen eye for outside investments
—banks, mines, lumber, textiles, railroads, real estate,
and so on. In some of these ventures Woolworth participated. He always insisted Knox was the best business man of the group but in the five-and-ten game,
without a dissenting murmur, Frank Woolworth himself was the acknowledged bellwether.

There were also many unfriendly competitors.

The bitterest of these had been young Herbert G.
Woolworth, brother of Fred, who had elected to remain
with Cousin Frank. Herbert, however, after a brief
apprenticeship in the Woolworth Syndicate, branched
out for himself; he opened red fronts in Boston, Worcester, Rochester, Albany and elsewhere; and publicly
avowed his intention of competing in every town
tapped by the Woolworth Syndicate. As nearly as he
could make them, Herbert's stores were replicas of the
familiar Woolworth red fronts and F. W. never forgave
him for this and for use of the name.

Other rivals were McCrory, with a dozen stores in
the Middle West; the Titus Supply Company in Pennsylvania; H. Germain in New Jersey and New York;
Rothchild & Company in New York; and two men of
whom much was to be heard later; Sebastian S. Kresge
and Samuel Henry Kress. With a partner, Kresge, a
former farm boy and hardware salesman, operated a
large five-and-ten in Pittsburgh, and smaller ones elsewhere. Bold, able and persistent, he was destined to

become Woolworth's chief detestation. S. H. Kress owned a number of stores in the South. He was a more amicable opponent, having been shepherded in the five-and-ten game by Fred Kirby. They had met when Kress, a pleasant young man of old American stock, ran a small stationery store on East Market Street, Wilkes-Barre.

Individually, none of these rivals threatened Woolworth seriously, yet collectively they were worrisome. Because of their adoption of some of his distinctive features in color scheme and arrangement, Woolworth often had considered legal action but was deterred by the fact that competition frequently spurred his own sales and profits. Sometimes the blooming of a second red front made communities more five-and-ten conscious and created a demand never known before. This was one of the mysteries of the five-and-ten business.

But when, in 1905, there was a rumor of a $5,000,000 anti-Woolworth combination, led by the men and firms above mentioned, Woolworth sprang into action. He knew that he had resources and buying advantages that no competitor could match, and he outlined the following methods of attack:

Scheme No. 1—When your competitor puts a line of goods in his window, pick out the best selling items in these goods and put them in your window at just half his price; and keep them there just as long as he keeps similar goods in his window.

Scheme No. 2—In another window, without any advertising or fuss, put a special line of goods costing from $14.40 to $36.00 per gross wholesale. Inside your store put these goods on a small counter in the rear, just as though they were regular daily bargains, and have but one girl waiting on the counter no matter how many customers appear. Keep a showing of these special, high-priced goods continually in your quiet window.

Scheme No. 3—The same special goods should be displayed at least once a week by stores that have no competition simply to brace up trade.

Soon the war was on and the Woolworth stores were selling unprecedented bargains at ten cents, among them oil stoves, coffee mills, bucksaws, wash bowls and pitchers, camp chairs, clothes baskets, umbrellas, lace curtains, bed blankets, nightgowns, overalls, men's white and colored shirts and even women's shirt waists and white skirts and children's dresses.

Out in the field the conflict raged right merrily and the boys reported the skirmishes to New York headquarters. Here is a typical letter from H. H. Albright, the ex-postman, then manager at Pittsburgh:

May 8, 1905.

We had our first real battle with Kresge & Wilson Saturday night after the store closed and while it cost money we feel we won out. As I wrote you Saturday, we trimmed with import china salad dishes, big jugs and chocolate pots. Finished about 10.30 P.M. and Mr. Newberry and I boarded a car for home. As we passed Kresge & Wilson's store, I noticed the lights were all out, everything dark, but saw persons moving about in one of the windows. We jumped off the car and peeked. K & W had begun trimming with fine china chocolate pots (larger and just as fine as ours), china cuspidors, olive dishes etc. Wilson and Kirkberger were doing the trimming. We returned to our store and found John Downey, the window trimmer, and Red McKenzie, the candy man. They had learned K & W were putting in chocolate pots. We immediately changed all tickets in our window to 5 cents, then stood in a dark doorway until Wilson and Kirkberger came past on their way home. You should have seen the effect. Wilson was smoking a "toby" and the sparks fairly flew. They went back and changed their price to 5 cents. While they were doing that, we put 2 for 5 signs on ours. It was nearly 2 A.M. now and Wilson and Kirkberger went back and put 2 for 5 signs in their window. We cut ours to 4 for 5, then watched and waited half an hour or so. But they made no further move, so we went home.

A new and aggressive buyer, Walter Williams, was placed in charge of competition sales and Woolworth ordered his managers to go at the enemy "with double energy and force":

Don't be afraid to lose a little money. First, it prevents your competitor from making money; second, it advertises our stores more than anything else could do and will make people talk about us for years to come. We have had fights like this before and have always come out on top.

Many of the stores showed losses for a time but gradually competition weakened. One rival changed from a five-and-ten to a twenty-five-cent store.

Then came the Panic of 1907, which shook the country's entire commercial fabric. The smaller rivals went down like ninepins. The first failure was that of H. Germain. Woolworth refused a receiver's request to bid on the Germain stores. He did, however, bid in three Illinois stores belonging to the liquidated firm of Holmes, Tolle & Evans.

Then, in 1908, Herbert G. Woolworth & Company collapsed. Herbert had battled courageously to the end, with only five stores remaining. The others he had sold the previous fall to Sebastian S. Kresge, who had incorporated as Kresge & Company and was spreading out.

Woolworth noted Herbert's failure with relish, for he had never forgiven this rebellious member of the family for what he considered misuse of the name. Herbert faded from the five-and-ten field and went into the baking business in the Middle West.

Though the anti-Woolworth $5,000,000 combination did not materialize, Woolworth was on his guard and more determined than ever before to place his stores uppermost in the mind of the public. He instructed his managers to send to the New York office samples of 20- and 25-cent articles sold in other stores so that these could be duplicated by manufacturers working with him. Learning that Clark's ONT and Coates' thread were placing a minimum retail price of six cents on their product, he sent out confidential instructions to his men:

> The companies will not sell us direct unless we agree to the 6 cts. price. Now, this is the opportunity of a life time, the biggest advertisement we can get at this time. So keep very quiet about it but buy all the spool cotton you can from jobbers or retailers, even if you have to pay 75 cents a dozen; and sell it for five cents.

Soon the coveted spool cotton bloomed on red front counters at five cents. The manufacturers were furious but their protests were futile and Woolworth's stores reaped the sort of advertising he considered most valuable.

Woolworth was ever alert to give the public a good buy for a dime and was always willing to stand a temporary loss for the sake of enhanced prestige. Lewis E. Pierson, honorary chairman of the Irving Trust Company, tells of an incident illustrating the merchant's business acumen:

During this period Pierson, then president of the Irving National Exchange Bank, of which Woolworth had become a director, was invited to accompany the five-and-ten man to Lancaster for a gala reopening of Woolworth's still larger pioneer store. The evening before the opening, Woolworth escorted the banker for a walk about the town. Passing a hardware store, Woolworth spied a display of lanterns at fifty cents each.

"There are our big leaders for tomorrow!" he exclaimed. "Watch me."

He bustled into the store, bought out the entire stock of lanterns which next morning glistened in the five-and-ten's main show window under a sign: "Ten Cents—While They Last! One To a Customer."

"Woolworth lost forty cents each on those lanterns," comments Mr. Pierson, "but the advertising value was worth the difference. Every farmer around Lancaster knew the lanterns were worth half a dollar and you ought to have seen them gape when the lanterns were offered at a dime."

At the same time Woolworth knew when not to attract attention to his stores. Informed that one manager was stamping packages with the name of his store, he peremptorily directed:

"Have all the signs you want inside and outside our stores but under no circumstances send out any pack-

age with our name on it. We don't want Mrs. Brown
to know that Mrs. Jones has been shopping in the five
and ten and Mrs. Jones doesn't want to advertise to
Mrs. Brown that she has to go to a five and ten cent
store to buy her goods. It might look like she is hard
up."

Losses through theft were a bothersome problem.
To impress upon his men the need of constant watch-
fulness, Woolworth one day assumed the role of
Raffles.

Slipping into half a dozen of his metropolitan stores,
without making any effort to disguise himself, he stole
everything in sight. In the first store he dropped 300
picture post cards into his outside overcoat pocket.
Strolling along, unrecognized, he crammed other
pockets with doll dresses, baby ribbon, cakes of soap,
rubber balls, stick pins, bow ties, even a claw hammer.
In three minutes he had stolen $10 worth of goods.
These he dumped upon the desk of a dumbfounded
manager and remarked acidly: "I could have filled a
delivery truck." In another store he asked to have a
pair of eye-gless frames fitted and, as the sales girl
did not seem attentive, walked away with the frames
on his nose. The dramatic experiment resulted in new
and drastic regulations.

With the number of his stores approaching 300, and
drawing prodigally upon his energies to run them,
Woolworth's health in 1911 was none too stable. He
had never quite recovered from an attack of influenza
two years before. He had grown noticeably stouter (he
weighed 237 pounds) and more flabby. He scorned exercise in any form and at all hours of the day and night
indulged a fondness for rich foods—lobster, rarebits,
etc. He doted upon bananas, a delicacy of which he
had been deprived in youth, and preferred them overripe. He became irritable and suspicious.

"Mr. Woolworth was the most notional individual I ever knew," recalls Beecher Winckler, his first confidential secretary, who went to work for him in 1911. "He wanted to have a finger in every pie, to know what every man in his organization was doing. He used to go poking around among the buyers' offices and desks, looking in corners and examining packages, especially around the holidays, to make sure none of them violated the rule against presents or 'souvenirs' from manufacturers.

"While Mr. Woolworth had built up a magnificent business organization, he was at this time highly unsystematic about his own finances. Sometimes he would hold checks for weeks before depositing them. Once, when $212,000 in perfectly good checks had accumulated in his wallet, I said to him: 'Mr. Woolworth, would you walk to the window every morning and toss twelve dollars and fifty cents into the street?' 'Of course not, young man.' 'Well,' I told him, 'that's the amount you're losing in interest every day by failing to deposit those checks.' He looked at me as though in complete surprise and, without a word, pulled the checks out and handed them over.

"Yet he could be as careful in matters involving small amounts as he was careless with large sums. Once he missed a quarter from his change pocket and thought it must have rolled under the couch or in a corner. He and I and the little French-Canadian porter remained long after closing time searching unsuccessfully for it."

Though Woolworth loved to pick quarrels, there was one man he seldom tried to ruffle. This was the indomitable Peck, his right bower, who stood like a mighty mastiff guarding the interests of the business. A favorite, too, was a hustling new buyer, C. T. Newberry, who was boosting the new sheet-music department. Handsome Charlie Newberry was the most eligible bachelor among the executives and all the girls in the office cast sheep's eyes at him. Eventually he married C. P. Case's daughter, Anna. Later, with his brother, he founded the J. J. Newberry chain of variety stores. He died in 1939.

Another man whom Woolworth, strange to say, never sought to roil was his swashbuckling Franco-Swiss chauffeur, Jules Billard. Jules was now wed to Mlle. Ducharme, a member of the Metropolitan Opera cast; and in his "motor department" he had an assistant chauffeur, Schmelz, and two handsome Renault cars to look after in addition to the Panhard, which was kept in Europe.

Along about April of each year Jules awaited orders to sail in advance of the boss, condition the Panhard, and map out the summer's touring schedule.

This year, 1911, the order was delayed. For the biggest event in five-and-ten history was brewing.

In the spring of 1911 five sober-minded and pros-perous-looking gentlemen were seated at a table in the old Waldorf Astoria Hotel in New York City. They were Knox, Kirby, Charlton, C. S. and Frank Wool-worth—the friendly rivals of the five-and-ten.

They had foregathered, as they often did, to dis-cuss their business.

On this occasion, however, they were faced with the definite problem of how each of them could con-tinue to expand his individual chain without over-lapping on the other. Spreading out fanwise, their stores now blanketed the country—and there was very real danger that they would blanket each other. Already there had been several incidents of young am-bitious men in their various organzations bidding against one another for new leases and outlets.

Knox now controlled 112 stores; Kirby, 96; Charlton, 53; C. S. Woolworth, 15; while Frank Woolworth topped them all with 318. They all wished to continue to expand. They talked long and earnestly. And then Frank Woolworth exclaimed:

"Tell you what would solve the problem—a merger!"

He was putting into words what had been his dream for a long time.

To the others, the idea was a little breath-taking. They parted for the day to meet next day at the Hotel Plaza.

The meetings continued until late in June. The conferees had by this time agreed that to merge their various holdings into one company was, in the main, the logical thing to do. It would increase their efficiency, both in buying and selling, their financial strength—and probably their profits. It would give them a solid base from which to ward off any competitors and upon which to build for the future. Though none of them liked to admit it, they were advancing in years. Woolworth, the oldest, was nearing sixty; the rest were in their fifties; and there was that chance, if anything happened to them, that their enterprises might fall into the wrong hands. Among the five, there were singularly few male heirs who could be expected to carry on.

Yet there were many difficulties requiring compromise, concession and further discussion. One stickler was Frank Woolworth's insistence that the merged companies should bear his name. This was logical inasmuch as he, the pioneer, controlled more stores than all the others combined and possessed by far the most valuable trade-mark.

The other men, each proud of his life's work, winced at first at the idea of submerging their individual identities. Finally they agreed. It was agreed also that the merger, if finally decided upon, should take the form of a stock corporation with the holdings distributed to each group on a basis of capital invested and net income produced. With this understanding, the principals adjourned June 20 to meet again in the fall.

In September the five men again met in New York and worked out the details of their merger.

The corporation agreement was signed on the afternoon of Thursday, November 2; and Woolworth gave out a brief statement:

> F. W. Woolworth announces that a corporation is about to be formed with a capital stock of $65,000,000, of which $15,000,000 will be preferred stock and $50,000,000 common. This corporation will take over the business of F. W. Woolworth & Company of New York City; S. H. Knox & Company of Buffalo, N. Y.; F. M. Kirby & Company of Wilkes-Barre, Pa.; E. P. Charlton & Company of Fall River, Mass.; C. S. Woolworth of Scranton, Pa; W. H. Moore of Watertown, N. Y.; and W. H. Moore & Son of Schenectady, N. Y.
>
> Goldman, Sachs & Company of 60 Wall Street, New York, are the brokers in the transaction, who will market the stock. The name of the new corporation will be the F. W. Woolworth Company. It will probably be incorporated under the laws of the state of New York and will own over 600 five and ten cent stores throughout the United States, Canada and England.

Woolworth, it will be noted, had not forgotten his old mentor, Moore, for whom he had been buying goods all these years.

Now five-and-ten had really become Big Business; and was so hailed in the press.

The new corporation's stock—of which the $15,000,-000 preferred represented tangible physical assets, and the $50,000,000 common, good will and future earning possibilities—was to be listed on the New York Stock Exchange and abroad. After many consultations, and upon the advice of Woolworth's banker friend, Lewis Pierson, the firm of Goldman, Sachs & Company was selected to handle the stock and give it a world-wide market. This firm interested other leading houses in the underwriting, including Kuhn, Loeb & Co., Lehman Brothers, Speyer & Co., Lazard Frères and Ladenburg, Thalmann.

The prospectus listed the sales of the combined companies for the preceding five years as: 1906, $27,291,108.55; 1907, $32,434,895.67; 1908, $35,677,-553.94; 1909, $43,924,962.88; 1910, $50,345,646.15—a healthy and rapid growth.

In the new corporation, F. W. Woolworth held an interest of something over fifty per cent; Knox and Kirby about fifteen per cent each; Charlton ten per cent; and C. S. Woolworth about five per cent.

The negotiations had been conducted so quietly that most managers read of it first in the newspapers. Woolworth reassured them:

"The new company will take charge January 1, 1912. By next spring we will wind up the old companies by exchange of old stock for new. You will be offered 7% cumulative preferred stock in exchange for your present 7% stock in F. W. Woolworth & Company.

"We intend to make as few changes as possible," he added. "You will receive as much income as formerly. There will be eight district offices in this country and Canada and we have endeavored to mix the men from the various companies so as to make the organization as harmonious as possible and avoid friction. Please refrain from criticism."

New York remained general executive headquarters; the other district offices were located in Boston, Wilkes-Barre, Buffalo, Chicago, St. Louis, San Francisco and Toronto. The number of buyers in New York was increased to nineteen, with the addition of nine Knox, Kirby and Charlton aides. Among the Knox veterans was Edwin Merton McBrier, the Knox and Woolworth first cousin who, as we have seen, had been an early associate of the two in Lockport, New York. McBrier, temporarily quitting trade, had sailed for China in 1890 as a Methodist missionary aboard a tiny Canadian Pacific freighter. Later, returning to the United States on furlough, he married and rejoined Knox in the five-and-ten business, without, however, ever losing touch with his religious and philanthropic work in China. Today he is the patron saint of the university in China which bears the name Yenching.

Of the new district managers two, Ralph Connable (Toronto) and Seymour Knox's younger brother, Henry D. (Buffalo), had long been right-hand men to Knox; F. J. Weckesser (Wilkes-Barre), an old North Country boy, was Kirby's chief dependable; and E. A. Bardol (Boston) had been for years with Charlton. The others, C. P. Case (New York), C. C. Griswold (Chicago), Lambert G. Smith (St. Louis) and William J. Rand, Jr. (San Francisco), were all F. W. Woolworth men.

The Frank Woolworth group also dominated the executive offices. F. W. Woolworth became president and Carson Peck, retaining his post of general manager, became also a vice president with the remaining four founders: Knox, Kirby, Charlton and C. S. Woolworth. W. H. Moore was elected honorary vice president, H. T. Parson secretary-treasurer, and C. F. Valentine accountant.

The merger moved one manager, D. W. Doerr of

Knox's Milwaukee store, to pen a parody of Kipling's "L'envoi":

> When earth's last ten-cent store has opened
> And the new painted red front has dried
> And the oldest clerk has her station
> Down near the register's side,
> We will look to new worlds to sell to
> Perhaps Jupiter, Venus or Mars
> And the master of all the ten-cent stores
> Will put us to work in the stars.

Not so poetic was General Manager Peck, who reminded the augmented corps of buyers:

"The success or failure of the new company rests with you. You are not simply buyers; you are merchants. The great thing in buying is to get as near the source of supply as possible. You are expected not only to buy but to know that what you buy is sold. You are not only responsible for the purchase but for the *sale* and *profit* of the lines assigned to you."

Quick to sniff a bargain, the boys on the New York Curb Exchange began to trade from hand to hand in the new corporation's stock "if and when issued." These agile entrepreneurs ran the preferred up to $109 a share and the common to $84. Woolworth moved to protect his men, offering each manager up to twenty shares of common stock at $50 and each executive employee up to one hundred shares. He warned, however, that purchasers must not expect any dividends on the common for at least a year.

Well within that period, the common was paying 5 per cent; and within little more than a decade each of the $50 common shares was worth $1,000 and had earned triple its face value in dividends. This was because the volume of sales, ergo profits, was running vastly beyond the $75,000,000 mark which the founders estimated as the ultimate limit.

At an organization meeting in February, 1912, twenty directors were elected, including three bankers: Henry Goldman, A. Barton Hepburn, and Philip Lehman; also an executive committee of seven: the five founders plus Messrs. Peck and Parson. A nominal salary of $25,000 per year was fixed for President F. W. Woolworth and $10,000 each for the vice presidents. Resolutions were adopted retiring store managers at fifty-five and office executives at sixty. This rule, with occasional exceptions has been enforced since.

As a matter of sentiment, Watertown was selected as the home office. Just before the new corporation took over, W. H. Moore, retiring, wrote Woolworth:

> Friend Frank: Yesterday I turned over to the new company the keys I have held for more than fifty-five years with feelings of gratitude to you for the honors you have been instrumental in heaping upon me, which I am unable to express in words. I will watch with the greatest interest the workings of the F. W. Woolworth Company, more, if possible, than when a five and ten cent merchant. When three score years and ten covers your head, I pray that you may be as happy as I am,
>
> Gratefully yours,
>
> W. H. Moore

With 611 stores in three countries, the new corporation got off to a splendid start in 1912. Not so Woolworth. His nervous system was balking again, and this time dangerously. Insomnia afflicted him. Blasts of irritability met those who ventured to differ with him in the slightest particular, either at home or down-town.

One day Harry Albright, now earning $40,000 to $50,000 a year in salary and commissions as a buyer, bustled in proud as a peacock in a new fur coat. He showed it to everybody, and finally to Woolworth, who observed:

"A fine coat, Harry. Where did you buy it?"

"At Jaeckel's."

"And what did you pay for it?"

"Nine hundred dollars."

Woolworth paused a moment, then asked softly:

"Harry, did you ever stop to think that if it hadn't been for me, you wouldn't have a nice overcoat but would still be delivering mail in Lancaster?"

The buyer's jaw dropped, his face crimsoned, then he stammered: "Not a day goes by, Mr. Woolworth, that Mrs. Albright and I do not remember the opportunity you gave us," and rushed from the room.

Such wounds cut deep, though Woolworth often would seek to heal them by some unexpected act of kindness or generosity.

On February 1, the Woolworths' remaining daughter, Jessie, was married at the Fifth Avenue home to James Paul Donahue, a dapper engaging young Irish-American whose father supported a large family on New York's West Side by rendering fats and hides. The morning of the wedding Woolworth lay upon the couch in his office and his sobs could be heard far down the corridor. Those in the office thought he was merely upset emotionally over losing a loved daughter. But the cause was deeper. For some time his nervous debility had manifested itself in uncontrollable fits of weeping.

The attacks continued and in April the merchant

collapsed and was put to bed under the care of
nurses. His weight had dropped alarmingly; his joints
became swollen and stiff. A consultation of specialists
in nervous diseases informed him bluntly that he
could live not more than two years at the pace he was
traveling and recommended complete rest and treat-
ment in Carlsbad, Austria, adding:

"If you take care of yourself and obey orders, you
may be good for another fifteen years."

Thoroughly frightened, Woolworth agreed to accept
the verdict and sailed for Europe on May 14, accompanied by his second daughter, Edna Hutton, and her
husband, two nurses and a newly hired valet, Joseph.
Mrs. Woolworth and other members of the family
were forbidden to make the trip, as the doctors wanted
no one along who would give the invalid too much
sympathy.

Woolworth remained in Carlsbad six weeks, drink-
ing the hot "sprudel" and "schlossbrunnen" waters,
and taking radium baths, electric treatments, and so
on. But he was still tortured by insomnia, and his
weight continued to drop. Few letters were permitted,
for mere sight of familiar handwriting brought on a
flood of tears.

Nevertheless, Woolworth's sense of humor never
quite deserted him. One evening roars of laughter
came from the merchant's suite in the Imperial hotel—
the night nurse, trying to cheer him, had told him the
story of an old maid crying her eyes out on the shores
of a lake and explaining: "If I had been married and
had children, I just know every one of them would
have been drowned in this lake."

Thereafter, mere mention of the old maid would
bring a burst of merriment from the patient.

Chauffeur Jules and the Panhard arrived and in July
Woolworth was driven to Marienbad, thirty-two miles

away, for the "after cure." Here he was attended by
the famous Dr. Ott, who had been King Edward's
physician, and who told him that with care he'd recover from his illness in a year and a half.

"But you won't recover," said the blunt old nerve
specialist, "unless you obey orders. Don't be like King
Edward. He insisted on riding in rainy and cold
weather in open carriages and contracted pneumonia.
That was the real cause of his death."

Mrs. Hutton was expecting a baby later in the year
(the infant who was to become Woolworth's most publicized grandchild, Barbara); so she and her husband
returned to America. Woolworth cabled frantically for
his wife, and Mrs. Woolworth left on two days' notice,
escorted by her brother-in-law, Alvin Ivie. When they
arrived in Marienbad they found Cousin Fred Woolworth with the patient, and Fred was worried.

"Indeed, Woolworth seemed weak and ill," recollects Ivie. "But he had enough life in him to keep his
nurses at constant odds. He would tell each nurse
what the other thought and said about her, pure in-
ventions, and Mrs. Woolworth and I found the nurses
at such loggerheads that they refused to speak to one
another."

In August the Woolworths and one of the nurses,
Miss Salter, who was to remain with Woolworth the
rest of his life, left Marienbad for a motor tour of
Switzerland and France. The tour seemed to do the
patient more good than the treatments.

Feeling much better, he returned to America and
went at once to a rented house on Long Island. But
the dreaded insomnia returned, and October found
him on his way back to Europe.

After a brief tour of Spain, he settled for a while
in Pau. Here, in the snow-clad Pyrenees, Woolworth's
nerves and general health seemed to improve.

He improved so much, indeed, that early in December he determined to return to New York and push through an undertaking that meant even more to him than the great $65,000,000 merger—the erection in New York of the tallest skyscraper in the world.

Chapter XII

The Cathedral of Commerce

ON A SOFT spring evening in 1913 an unaccustomed stream of limousines and carriages flowed into the business district of lower New York. Their occupants alighted at a Broadway corner.

By seven o'clock, some eight hundred men prominent in the arts and letters, science and industry, law and politics were assembled in an improvised banquet hall.

Thirty minutes later, the lights were lowered. There was a moment of hushed silence as the recently inaugurated President of the United States, Woodrow Wilson, pressed a button in Washington. Instantly 80,000 electric bulbs in New York were set aglow; and from the blackness of the mild, moonless spring night there sprang into sparkling life the world's tallest and most beautiful skyscraper—the highest habitable structure ever reared by man.

In the banquet hall a concealed orchestra broke into the strains of the national anthem. Leaping to their feet, the diners cheered and toasted the very stout elderly gentleman with white mustache and impish blue eyes, who was their host.

The toastmaster, F. Hopkinson Smith, noted novelist and painter, addressed the assemblage.

"Gentlemen," he said, " a new man has come to the front. An all-round American this man: born on a farm up our state; clerk behind the counter of a cross-road country store the year he voted; without capital; without friends at first; working eighteen hours out of the twenty-four and still at it. This building, a thing of beauty, is a lasting monument to a plain farmer boy who has kept ahead of the procession."

To host Frank Woolworth, this night was the proudest of his sixty-one years. For this cloud-caressing sky-scraper, which carried not a scrap of indebtedness, was entirely his, erected on nickels and dimes, a Niagara of nickels and dimes.

And this is how it had all come about.

For many years Woolworth had nursed the idea of erecting an outstanding building that would bear his name. Each time he visted London he would stand, rapt in admiration, before the spirelike structures of the great houses of parliament, the rich Gothic architecture of which pleased him more than any other. Some day, he told himself, he would erect a structure even more impressive.

The first Woolworth Building in Lancaster only served to spur his ambition. The real Woolworth Building was to be in New York and to house the home offices of the five and ten.

By 1909 he had acquired a plot at the corner of Broadway and Park Place through a real estate broker, Edward J. Hogan. His first idea was to put of an imposing structure of perhaps twelve stories maybe sixteen. And then, not to be dwarfed by the golden-domed Pulitzer Building across City Hall Park, he envisioned twenty.

While his thoughts were thus soaring, he invited
Lewis Pierson, his young banker friend, to lunch with
him one day at the Hardware Club. They were old associates, these two, having first met in 1898 when Pierson was cashier of the New York National Exchange
Bank on the second floor of the Gerkin Building at
West Broadway and Chambers street, and Woolworth
a depositor. Since then, Pierson's career had been
as meteoric as Woolworth's own. He had risen to the
presidency of the National Exchange, and in 1906
engineered its merger with the Irving National Bank
—a union which was to develop into the present huge
Irving Trust Company. The merged institution, the
Irving National Exchange, became widely known as
the "bill of lading" bank because of its extensive transactions with large wholesale firms that used bills of
lading as a basis of credit. Now Pierson was guiding
the bank through a period of rapid expansion; and
Woolworth, an influential director, backed his every
move.

Hence the men were in jovial mood when they met
at the Hardware Club. This club, founded by the
late John W. Mackay in 1894 atop his new Postal
Telegraph Building at 253 Broadway, was Woolworth's
favorite noontime resort. For years he and his men sat
at a conspicuous round table in the dining room. The
table always groaned under steaming platters of food,
for the five-and-ten executives had never forgone the
heavy midday meals of their youth.

On this occasion, after enjoying his usual hearty
luncheon, Woolworth came to what was on his mind.
Would the Irving Bank be interested in leasing a floor
or two in his proposed building as a permanent home?
Pierson thought it would, decidedly.

After luncheon, the two men walked along the west
border of City Hall Park and Woolworth pointed out

the site he had purchased. Pierson was enthusiastic. And as Woolworth looked south and beheld a few blocks away the towering Singer Building, its summit 612 feet from the pavement, he murmured, almost as much to himself as to his companion:

"Perhaps we can get more land and raise her higher than twenty stories."

Within a few months, the hustling Hogan had obtained additional land, giving Woolworth a frontage of 105 feet on Broadway and 197 feet on Park Place.

At this point Woolworth consulted and retained the architect, Cass Gilbert, whose classic designs in stone were fast bringing him fame. A self-made man, as was Woolworth, Cass Gilbert had designed the New York Custom House, the Minnesota State Capitol and other noted buildings. He seemed to catch richness and warmth, as well as beauty and grandeur—qualities which so fascinated Woolworth in the Houses of Parliament buildings, and which he wanted reproduced in his structure. The five-and-ten man's choice of Gilbert as his architect turned out to be a stroke of genius.

Woolworth instructed Gilbert at their first meeting that the building must be "at least forty stories hight." Finally, by adding two more floors, they were able to top the Singer Building by 13 feet.

However, New York boasted another skyscraper, 88 feet higher than the Singer Building. This was the 700-foot Metropolitan Tower, the tallest habitable structure in the world, some two miles to the north of Woolworth's proposed new landmark.

Now it seemed to Woolworth that everywhere he went, in Europe as well as America, he saw picture post cards, magazine articles, and heard people talking of the glories of the Metropolitan Tower. It began bothering him that his name should be attached merely to the world's second highest skyscraper; and at the same time his vanity was fired by that acute business sense which never deserted him: the enormous advertising value and prestige of a building which would be the world's tallest.

So, parcel by parcel, he acquired more land until he owned the entire block front on Broadway and sufficient depth on Barclay Street as well as Park Place to put up a structure that would top all others.

Now he asked for bids on the actual construction. After a keen tussle, the contract was landed by Louis J. Horowitz, president of the Thompson-Starrett Company.

Because of the Woolworth Building's record height, unique construction and engineering problems had to be faced and solved by architect and builders. The foundation for all columns had to be carried down to solid bed rock, some 120 feet below the earth's surface, without disturbing the labyrinth of pipes, tubes, wires and sewers lying beneath the streets of New York. By means of the pneumatic caisson process, metal tubes (some 19 feet in diameter) were sunk through soil, mud, silt and water. Upon reaching bed rock, each tube (there were sixty-nine in all) was gradually filled with concrete, thus forming solid concrete piers upon which to rest the steel columns of the building. At the caisson base the total load on the rock was 24 tons per square foot. The building's weight above the caissons, including allowance for wind pressure, was estimated at 223,000 tons. The structure could not rock in the slightest degree because the dead load on any of the columns was greater than maximum uplift due to wind pressure.

The steel framework began to show itself above the sidewalk November 15, 1911. Requiring 24,000 tons of structural steel, with no free storage outside the building lines, absolute precision was a necessity for the workers. Each huge beam of steel, punched, ready and numbered, heavy as a bridge truss and as thick, was hoisted from the trucks as required and swung into place.

The steel members were of such weight that even the routes along which they were borne to the site had to be carefully surveyed to prevent cave-ins. Hoisting equipment had to be devised more powerful than any in existence. Material was lifted halfway by powerful cable cranes, then relayed to a second hoisting machine. Similarly, steam and water pipes had to be manufactured larger and stronger than those ever made before.

"The greatest difficulty we had," remarks Louis Horowitz in his *The Towers of New York*, "was to prevent Mr. Woolworth making decisions that only specialists were fitted to make. I grew very fond of him, though. Often he took me to his Fifth Avenue home and played his electrical reproducing pipe organ, the ducts of which were cunningly placed throughout the palacelike interior. Sometimes he would play for hours, not stopping until he was relaxed and easy in his mind."

From his office across the park, Frank Woolworth watched the upward lift into the blue of his gigantic skeleton of steel with pride and elation that knew no bounds. He asked a thousand questions. How could the tower be protected from wind strains? By means of portal braces, such as those used at bridge ends, which transmitted the wind successively downward until it reached the foundation. Good. And how was the danger of lightning to be avoided? Through copper cables linking the copper roofs of the main building and tower with the structural steelwork and "grounding the structure" with an effect similar to the ordinary lightning conductor. Fine.

The owner wanted a hand in every sub-contract, of which there were hundreds, but after one or two costly mistakes he permitted the builders and Cass Gilbert to supervise these. Indeed, he finally developed so much confidence in Messrs. Gilbert and Horowitz that he flung wide the pursestrings upon the slightest recommendation from either. He paid cash on the line for everything, just as he was accustomed to do in his business.

He had been disappointed but not frustrated when Henry Goldman, of Goldman, Sachs & Company, had refused to permit the building project to be treated as a part of the $65,000,000 merger's capital stock enterprise. Goldman believed the building, however profitable, would be merely an excrescence on the Woolworth business and disturbing to investors. Woolworth contended it would be not only a sound investment of corporate funds but would advertise the company "for nothing." Goldman opposed, Woolworth insisted, but the banker won. This was Woolworth's first taste of what it would be like to share with others the control of the busines he had founded. He didn't like it. But he was determined there should be a great skyscraper telling the world that Frank Woolworth was a great man. So, as he good-humoredly informed Henry Goldman, he would build it with his own money, pay for it as he had always paid for goods—with cash. As a result, the building carried not a penny of mortgage or other obligation. It is doubtful if any operation of comparable magnitude has ever been carried through, before or since, so completely free of indebtedness.

The cash payments saved Woolworth many hundreds of thousands of dollars in discounts upon the enormous amounts of material required: 17,000,000 bricks, 7,500 tons of terra cotta, 28,000 tons of hollow tile, 87 miles of electric wiring, 53,000 pounds of bronze and iron hardware, 12 miles of marble wainscoting, etc.

Into the enterprise, including special and lavish interior decorations, he poured the enormous sum of $13,500,000—yet lived to see his investment paying upward of 6 per cent. For many years the income from the observation gallery alone, at the fifty-fourth floor, averaged $200,000 a year from the throngs of sightseers who came to view New York and the surrounding country from this matchless vantage.

When doubt was expressed that he would be able to find tenants for his fifteen acres of office space, Woolworth chuckled.

"Businessmen," he observed, "will fall all over themselves to be able to say their offices are in the tallest building on earth."

His prediction proved true.

The five-and-ten magnate was so carried away with his colossus that he distributed pictures of the building, in various stages of completion, to all his stores and agencies, in Europe as well as America, with instructions to have them published as widely as possible. The business benefit, he was certain, was incalculable. Also, he could not forbear suggesting to Messrs. Gilbert and Horowitz that they waive or cut their fees in consequence of the prestige that would come to them through their connection with the world's tallest skyscraper. Such suggestions, however, were rebuffed with considerable firmness by the architect and builder.

On July 1, 1912, while Woolworth was lying ill in Carlsbad, the flag went up on top of the tower, signalizing the completion of the structural steelwork. Exactly ten months later the building was finished, unparalleled speed for such an operation.

The completed building was a superb Gothic renaissance structure of surpassing beauty, rising 792 feet from the pavement. By some magic of inspiriation, Cass Gilbert and his fellow draughtsmen had contrived a scale giving their gigantic creation the true Gothic quality of lace-in-stone. Never before had a cathedral effect been achieved in a building of this type. Woolworth's dream had come true.

In practical features, as well as beauty, the new skyscraper was unique. It was the first building to have its own power plant. The four huge Corliss engines installed in the subbasement could generate sufficient power to light a city of 50,000 people. Thus, so far as heat, light, ventilation and elevator power was concerned, the building was self-contained.

The main entrance on Broadway led into the main arcade.

The walls of the arcade were of marble quarried on the Isle of Skyros off the coast of Greece; and richly carved in pure Gothic design, which blended into a dome-ceiling of glass mosaic. The whole was illuminated with soft concealed lights. A wide marble staircase led to the main office of the Irving Bank. Woolworth had become so enamored of marble that he had wanted the entire exterior of the building lined with it. Structural engineers, however, shook their heads over the added weight; and Cass Gilbert achieved his brilliant lace-in-stone effect with terra cotta.

There were thirty high-speed elevators, operated faster than any hitherto known; two of them rose 700 feet from the ground floor to the fifty-fourth in one minute. Yet they were equipped with every conceivable safety device, from air cushions and speed governors to automatic shaftway locks. In addition, there was a dispatcher system and telephonic communication with each elevator.

The building was expected to house a population of 15,000 tenants and their employees. Its own force of 300 service men, recruited and trained ahead of time, was organized along departmental lines: fire, police, cleaning, repair, maintenance, etc. The permanent mechanical staff included electricians, plumbers and carpenters.

As the upper floors were opened, Woolworth explored them eagerly. One day he was showing his friend Frank Taft, the organist, over the building. The tower was still closed to all save workmen, but the two men made their way as far as they could by the elevator and stairs. Reaching the topmost landing, Taft noticed a ladder extending up to the small trap door which was open, and began climbing.

"Hey there! Where are you going?" called Woolworth, who was already puffing from the unaccustomed exercise.

"I'm going to see what's up there," replied Taft, with a grin.

As quick as a flash Woolworth rejoined:

"Wait a minute. I've never been up that far and I don't propose to let you go higher in this building than I go myself." And up the ladder he scrambled.

When the two men found themselves at the peak of the tower just below the roof, Woolworth proposed gleefully:

"Say, let's write our names up here."

"Both of us then scrawled our names on the rafters," recalls Mr. Taft, "and were as much puffed up with pride as though we were youngsters carving our names on a park bench or a tree."

The building was formally opened by President Wilson from Washington on the night of April 24,

1913. This presidential dedication of a commercial structure was unprecedented, and there was some criticism of Mr. Wilson's act. Also, the newspapers, which Woolworth had never used as an advertising medium for the five-and-ten, took little notice of the event.

Nevertheless, the occasion was resplendent. The guests included a large delegation of congressmen who had come from Washington on a special train provided by the host. When President Wilson in the White House pressed a button, America's new wonder sprang into vivid outline against the darkness of New York's skyline.

The banquet guests rose, waved napkins and cheered. Outside, in historic City Hall Park and in near-by streets, other thousands took up the cheers; while millions within a radius of many miles gasped in admiration at the building which the phrase-making divine, Rev. Dr. S. Parkes Cadman, was prompt to christen the "Cathedral of Commerce."

Among the celebrants in the dining hall were Woolworth's friends and business associates, old and new, including several men from whom he had bought goods in his struggling days. D. Arnould, the candy manufacturer, was among them.

The draughtsmen and artists of Cass Gilbert's staff sat together: Thomas R. Johnson, George H. Wells, John R. Rockart, Cass Gilbert, Jr. They were chuckling at Tom Johnson's joke in designing and placing in out-of-the-way niches in the main hall grotesque statuettes of Cass Gilbert, Lewis Pierson, Louis Horowitz and Woolworth himself. The grotesque of Woolworth showed the five-and-ten tycoon counting out nickels and dimes to pay for his building. Woolworth laughed to the point of tears when he saw the caricature; and ordered that it never be removed.

At other tables were men who had played important parts in the building.

While the diners enjoyed caviar and green turtle soup, guinea hen, terrapin and squab, and mellowed upon amontillado, *pontet canet* and Sunnyside port, growing four-leaf-clover plants were distributed as souvenirs. Then Woolworth was introduced as the first speaker.

He began his talk with a homely touch that was one of his charms. In the presence of Elbert Gary, Otto Kahn, Charles M. Schwab and other industrial and banking celebrities, he introduced the two men he said had given him his start: William H. Moore and Perry Smith.

"Gentlemen, what made this building possible?" asked Woolworth. "Over forty years ago I went to work to learn the drygoods business in Watertown, New York, with Moore & Smith. They taught me the first lesson in my mercantile career and I am very thankful to them. Gentlemen, these two men are here tonight and I want you all to know them. They are two of the people who helped make this building possible. Mr. Moore and Mr. Smith, stand up and show yourselves."

Blushing, but proud as peacocks, the small-town merchants rose and received a great ovation. Woolworth continued:

"I do not wish to be egotistical, but if I have had any ability it has been in the selection of good generals as managers of the little business that I started. It was a little business. It commenced with a five-cent nickel piece. The first manager that I selected was a man named C. S. Woolworth. I believe they call him my brother. C. S. Woolworth, please stand up."

Blushing a bit also, C. S. Woolworth, now a solidly

built man of fifty-six, with dark hair and mustache, rose to receive a round of applause.

Having broken the ice, Woolworth proceeded in a gale of elation to present his leading lieutenants. He next called upon Banker Pierson to take a bow, and the real estate broker, Edward Hogan, whom he announced was now the renting agent. Then he passed on to Messrs. Gilbert and Horowitz.

He said there had been much discussion as to the exact height of the building, so that a week before he had ordered absolute engineering measurements. This was the result:

On the Park Place corner, from the sidewalk to the top of the tower, 791 feet and one-half inch.

On the Barclay Street corner, 792 feet.

On the Broadway front, 791 feet 6 inches.

At the Park Place entrance, 792 feet 3 inches.

At the Barclay Street entrance, 793 feet 9 inches.

"Those figures make an average height of the tower of 792 feet 1 inch," he explained. "The foundations are 121 feet below the sidewalk to bed rock. Therefore, from the bottom of the foundations to the top of the tower is 913 feet 1 inch. And the height of the tower above sea level, high tide, is 947 feet 2 inches."

The owner said that to determine the number of floors in the building, over which there had been much confusion, he had recently walked from the tower to the sub-basement, and discovered there were sixty, adding:

"We could easily have made the building 79 stories high, allowing 10 feet to a floor, but there is no floor less than 11 feet high and some are over 20 feet. So hereafter this will be known as a sixty-story building."

The speaker concluded by presenting Mr. Gilbert with a gigantic silver loving cup embellished with an engraving of the building.

The entire twenty-fourth floor and part of the twenty-third were given over to the Woolworth Company executive offices. For his own private office Woolworth set aside a beautiful apartment on the twenty-fourth floor, thirty feet square, facing south and east. This he determined to make the richest, most imposing office in the world. What should be its general decor and motif?

The question was still puzzling him in June when he was again ordered to Europe to give his overtaxed nerves another period of absolute rest. This time he chose a fashionable cure in Divonne, France, some fifteen miles northeast of Geneva. For three weeks he lay in bed on a broad balcony overlooking Lake Geneva, and for an additional fortnight took a course of baths. There was no medicine, a concession for which he was profoundly grateful.

Late in July Mrs. Woolworth and her sister, Mrs. Wood, joined him and, piloted by the indispensable Jules, the party began a leisurely tour of Switzerland and France. Stopping one day in Compiègne, they visited Napoleon's Palace. Entering the famous Empire Room, it occurred to Woolworth in a flash that here was the answer to the problem of his own private office. He, too, would have an Empire Room, modeled upon Napoleon's, and furnished and decorated even more elaborately. Had not his friend (and supplier) Simmons, the hardware man, written him when the Woolworth Building was mounting to the sky: "I am addressing the Napoleon of Commerce"?

Yes, he, too, would have an Empire Room. That would make the boys sit up and take notice!

In Paris and, later, in New York, he called in antique and art dealers and decorators to carry out his plans. In a letter dated February 20, 1914, addressed to "all stores, United States, Canada and Great Britain,"

Woolworth described the result—"the handsomest office in the country and possibly the world":

The ceiling is cream white with embossed gold decorations.Wall panels and wainscoting are of Vert Campan marble from the North of Italy with pilasters of dark marble and Empire capitals covered with gold. There is also a 24 inch marble floor border around the room.

There are 8 panels in each door with bronze mountings made in Paris of mercury gilt. Each panel contains a bronze and gold mounted figure representing a wreath, a lyre, lion, lioness etc.

The mantel is of green Tyros marble with mercury gilt bronze ornaments. On the west wall is an oil portrait of Napoleon in his coronation robes copied directly from the picture at Versailles.

The desk is 3 feet 9 by 7 feet 6 of mahogany with gilt bronze mounts and green leather top with hand-tooled gilt edge, Empire design. On the desk are two very handsome Empire lamps with gold figures of Victory over the top. The ink well was bought in Paris and represents Napoleon on horseback in bronze. A smaller figure of Napoleon is a paper weight, 100 years old.

The arm chairs, side chairs, sofa etc., are of mahogany, highly ornamented, carved and gilded. Two large round-back arm chairs are copies of the famous Throne Chair in the Palace of Fontainebleau. These are carved and finished in old gold and upholstered in red, pink and gold handmade tapestry.

In the room is a life size bust of Napoleon in bronze, mounted on a mahogany pedestal with gold trimmings. It represents Napoleon posing as Julius Caesar. He liked to look as much like Caesar as possible, you know.

The crowning feature of the room, however, is a clock piece set on the mantel which is reported to have been given to Napoleon by the Emperor of Russia over 100 years ago. I picked this clock set up in Paris last October as well as the bust. The clock itself represents a picture of Cleopatra in gold. There are candelabras depicting Egyptian figures composed of a very rare marble called Malachite which is seldom seen outside of museums. The figures are mounted on Pofroi marble from Egypt which is also very rare.

There is also a beautiful fireplace capable of burning real wood or coal as the President of the Company sees fit. Various parties told me the room would be cold because of the marble covered walls; but the furniture and decorations make it as cosy an office as there is in the building.

Off the Empire Room is a nice little office for the secretary to the President, decorated very simply in cream and gold with a handsome rug and Empire furniture.

The bite of the Napoleonic bug did not in the least divert Woolworth's attention from business. The merger had proved an unqualified success. With much less friction than had been anticipated, the Knox, Kirby and Charlton chains had been absorbed into the Woolworth organization. The master of the Empire Room now headed the greatest retail mercantile organization in the country.

In 1912, the first working year of the consolidation,

sales were $60,557,767.79 for 611 stores; and the net profit was $5,414,798.90.

In this year also, far ahead of schedule, the corporation declared a dividend of 2½% on the common stock; and in 1913 common stockholders were paid 5½%. Despite this increase, the company found it possible to add $2,661,000 to its accumulated surplus. As high as 7¾% could have been paid, but the company's policy, outlined at its formation, was to put as much out of earnings as possible into real property until the $50,000,000 good-will account was wiped out.

It will be remembered that when the big merger took place only $15,000,000 of the $65,000,000 capitalization was in tangible assets. These mainly consisted of properties and merchandise on hand. Because, however, an enterprise such as Woolworth did not necessarily entail the outlay of large sums but instead made its profits by turning its capital over and over, the $50,000,000 item was added and listed as "good will." For instance, in 1913 the 683 five-and-tens were completely replenished five times with the year's total sales of $66,228,000 and profits at $6,461,000—a goodly percentage of interest on the $65,000,000 capitalization.

However, Woolworth was determined to wipe out this good-will item with more tangible assets, which was eventually accomplished by turning back some of the surplus profits each year into the business.

An idea of the huge turn-over of merchandise for 1913 is to be found in the following list: 27,576,000 pairs of hosiery; 12,000 gross of mouse traps; 300,000 gross of clothespins; 108,000 infants' dresses; 700,000 felt pillow tops; 10,000 gross of tin toys; 3,000 gross of baby pacifiers; 130,000 dozen bottles of peroxide of hydrogen; 186 tons of hairpins; 368,000 gross of pearl buttons; 144,000 dozen cakes of soap.

Sales of jewelry exceeded $2,500,000; of glassware and crockery, $1,250,000; of candy, $8,500,000. Goods bought abroad totaled $3,758,000; in the United States, $38,000,000.

The stores were shuffled or transferred so that approximately 100 each were placed under the supervision of the Manhattan, Wilkes-Barre, Boston, Buffalo and Chicago offices. No transfers were made in the other districts. C. C. Griswold was brought to New York to assist Peck, and J. F. Nutting succeeded him in Chicago.

Gradually the leading lines of merchandise were standardized. For instance, many of the store managers had complained for years over tricky and incompetent practices in the manufacture of muslin wear. Each shipment was "salted" with small-sized or shabby and inferior garments. Buyer E. M. McBrier consulted fashion catalogues and textile experts and drew up a Woolworth standard—the first of many— covering sizes, materials and patterns. These specified even the number of button holes and the quality of buttons required before the manufacturer could get on Woolworth's approved list. Also each garment was to be stamped with the individual maker's initial.

Most of the manufacturers kicked like steers over the new and rigid requirements, but came up to scratch rather than lose the large and lucrative Woolworth orders. The result was a notable increase in quality, sales—and profits.

This was the story all along the line. With popular sheet music now selling to the tune of $1,500,000 a year, buyer C. T. Newberry wrung a reduction from the music publishers from seven to six and one-half cents—and thus stepped up the percentage of Woolworth profits on this item from 42 to 54. Truly, this was a business in which even spinning fractions of a cent spelled appreciable profit.

Meanwhile, the wise boys in Wall Street made haste to invest in this long-concealed gold mine. Shortly after being listed in 1912 on the Stock Exchange, Woolworth common rose to 112. On a long decline which stocks experienced in 1913, it fell back into the 80's; but on an upturn in the fall the price again went above 100.

In December, 1913, Carson Peck, active executive manager of the enlarged company, offered the common to store managers at 90, with a limit of ten shares to each purchaser and a pledge to hold on to it for at least a year. One hundred and sixty-two managers bought 1,311 shares, and Peck told them:

"This is a sure investment. Don't sell it any more than you would sell your birthright. And don't be worried if it should go up or down ten, fifteen or even twenty points."

Peck also added: "Things look rosy for 1914."

Neither he nor any one else, for that matter, could foresee the outbreak in a few months of a war that would shake even so smooth-running an organization as the five-and-ten to its very foundation.

Chapter XIII

War

THE summer of 1914 found Woolworth and his wife in the Hotel Royal, Evian-les-Bains, in the province of Savoie, France. Here, in a luxurious suite overlooking beautiful Lake Geneva, he was enjoying his customary period of baths and rest when the European War broke out with paralyzing suddenness.

The Woolworths were marooned here and in Geneva for several weeks before sailing for home September 26 from Havre on the French liner *La France*.

The homeward passage was smooth, comfortable and without special incident except for a meeting with Anne Morgan, daughter of the financier, of whom Woolworth remarked:

"Miss Morgan has a charming personality and devotes much of her time taking care of young shop girls. She appears very enthusiastic about her work and wants me to give her some room in the Woolworth Building. Of course I had to consent to it."

The first Monday in October found the traveler back at his desk in the Empire Room grappling with war problems, and these were many. The English business was greatly handicapped, and was calling for help from America. In Germany, the Fuerth office was closed because all the help had gone to the front. The near-by Sonneberg warehouse and office reported a complete shutting down; every man employed, including Fritz Dressel, the manager, had been drawn into the army. The company had paid out more than $500,000 for merchandise purchased in Germany and Austria, none of which had been actually received in American ports. All told, 28,000 cases of goods were tied up, most of it in Rotterdam awaiting cargo space—and a permit from the British government, which was tightening its blockade.

The Woolworth accountant, C. F. Valentine, went to Washington and persuaded the British embassy to release 12,000 cases. A few months later Valentine journeyed to London to verify the contents of the other purchases; and succeeded in obtaining release of the remaining 16,000 cases.

However, this was not the cause of the greatest worriment at five-and-ten headquarters. Substitutes could be found for many of the curtailed imports. But, as war orders and scarcity of labor and raw materials sent manufacturers' costs up, up, up, Woolworth realized that his fixed price principle—a fetish with him—would undergo an acid test. One by one, other variety stores took on higher-priced lines simply because they could not obtain enough items to sell for five and ten cents. Woolworth alone stuck to its established price limit, save in territory west of the Missouri River and in Canada, where higher freight rates and (in Canada) a protective tariff had for some time forced a 15 cent top.

To maintain the fixed price principle, without reducing sales and profits, a world of ingenuity was required. A few examples will show how the five-and-ten men rose to the challenge.

Huge quantities of the well-known D. M. C. imported crochet cotton had been sold at ten cents. Then the war prevented its importation and threatened to make the ten-cent ball of crochet cotton a memory. Woolworth induced an American mill to make exclusively for it a similar product, equal in quality to D. M. C., and guaranteed the spinner against loss. Thus was launched a famous crochet cotton—"Woolco"—which soon attained immense popularity.

Celluloid dolls were off the market because nobody in America knew how to make them. A Woolworth foreign buyer stepped into the breach. On his trips abroad he had studied so closely the celluloid-doll process that he was able to show American manufacturers how they could profitably produce these dolls to retail at a dime. A similar triumph was scored with Christmas tree ornaments. Woolworth backed an American manufacturer in successful experiments to duplicate the foreign process; and soon millions of "made in U. S. A." tree ornaments were being turned out.

In this trying period, the close relationship which Woolworth had built up over the years with manufacturers brought dividends. They looked upon him as a wizard and were perfectly willing—nay, eager— to introduce new manufacturing techniques and processes in order to take advantage of the buying volume which he guaranteed. These men swore by the five-and-ten and helped it meet its troublous war problems.

Take, for example, Samuel Magid, proprietor of the Little Nemo Manufacturing Company of Providence, R. I.

In 1905, Sam Magid was a wholesaler, a jobber, selling inexpensive jewelry to retail jewelry stores and department stores. One of Woolworth's district superintendents wanted job lots suitable for a special sale in a new store in South Boston. At $13.50 a gross, Magid closed out everything left from his regular fall stock, selling cuff buttons, brooches, scarf pins, rings and other items. Most of it had been designed to sell at 25 cents and even 50 cents in the average independent store. But in the Woolworth sale in Boston it was offered—and quickly taken—at 10 cents. The Woolworth superintendent came back to see Magid; he wanted more of a particular item which had been literally snatched off the counters. It was a signet ring made to fit a baby's finger.

"Get hold of more rings, Magid."

"Yes. The manufacturer has never made them for a penny less than $13.50 a gross."

"But I told you: As a regular item that's too much; for a special sale, for a leader it's all right, but—"

"Listen to me: The price to you will be $10.50. Never before for so little, and only because of big orders we hope for."

What happened then will bring tears to Mr. Magid's eyes any time he thinks about it, after thirty-five years. He'll tell you: "He patted my back. He said: 'My boy, some day you'll be a big dealer and sell us tremendous quantities of goods. Because you are honest.' That's Woolworth's policy: to give business to reliable fellows."

There was one twentieth of a pennyweight of 12-carat gold in one of those tiny rings. The average baby has too little acid in its system to tarnish even a lightly gold-washed ring. Finally, as if they all belonged to an informal cooperative, there were 600,000 American babies each one of whom possessed one of those ten-cent rings. Other transactions followed and so, in 1912, when the merger occurred, Sam Magid became a manufacturer himself and a supplier of the Woolworth counters. When the World War cut off some European novelties, Magid and his Little Nemo designers were ready to go to work night or day to supply substitutes. Today his firm makes each year about 2,000 sample items, costume jewelry, novelties etc., out of which perhaps 1,200 are accepted.

All over America, when Europe was at war, there were hundreds of manufacturers delivering most of their product to Woolworth and striving to help him keep prices down. To them the chain-store counters meant the one mighty force that made mass production possible and profitable: sales volume.

Another young manufacturer who won the lasting friendship of the five-and-ten men during the war days was Max Rosenfield.

The variety of goods shipped from the Newark, N. J., and Long Island City factories of Max Rosenfield would bewilder the ordinary intellect. Fresh sample items are evolved daily. At any time of year his employees are making hundreds of things. But as today's molded plastic ring toy ceases to draw orders, it is succeeded by a fresh design in plastic poker chips or bracelets, bracelets that would have deluded wives of King Solomon into thinking the old boy had came into possession of some mighty fine new mines.

Max Rosenfield first went to call on a Woolworth buyer in celluloid the year the merger was consummated. He was about twenty, and with a few workmen in a loft was making cuff buttons of discs linked with loops of wire. He talked with B. H. Danks, one of the buyers.

"Frankly, young fellow, we don't have any sale for men's jewelry. Women's jewelry, yes. Loads of it."

"But, Mr. Danks, suppose each pair were displayed

on a card like this. Women would recognize their purpose, buy them for their husbands—maybe."

"Maybe—indeed," said the Woolworth buyer, sitting erect and writing on a pad. It was, young Rosenfield realized, an order pad! For a few seconds he thought he was already a rich man. There were more than 600 Woolworth stores. But what Mr. Danks handed to him was an order for only 21 stores, each order amounting to $4.21. Crestfallen, Rosenfield decided Mr. Danks had been right. A Woolworth store was not the place to sell men's jewelry. However, he filled the orders.

A few days later he received an order from one of the big stores: No. 13 in the Boston district. There were reorders from the first stores and so Rosenfield returned to the buyer. Mr. Danks waved him into a chair.

"I know all about it. Don't tell me. Look!" Spread on his desk were orders from hundreds of stores. Orders eventually totaled thousands and thousands of gross.

That marked the real beginning of Mr. Rosenfield's career as a Woolworth supplier. The item sold in the stores for years. The little factory's payroll grew steadily. Every three or four months Rosenfield and Danks would consider improvements, a touch of celluloid trim or some other change, each change kept simple so as not to interfere with the maker's ability to produce the cuff links at six cents a pair *profitably*.

That was the amazing thing! Woolworth buyers were striving to be as considerate of manufacturers' profits as their own! But when wartime competition became hot and Mr. Danks suggested cuff buttons could be made with mother-of-pearl blanks, with celluloid trim, chained together with gold-washed wire loops, Rosenfield thought: "Now they're going to sink me!"

However, Mr. Danks figured with him, and at $12 a gross, they found, Rosenfield could do it. That is a terrible price, as any retailer of ten-cent items knows, but the response was glorious! Eventually Mr. Rosenfield's factory was producing and making good money on a mother-of-pearl center, gold-plated cuff link for $10.80 a gross, and he says today that when he began he would have supposed he had to charge three times as much or more to break even. Today, thanks to his understanding of the cost-reducing power in volume and an astonishing manufacturing flexibility gained by using plastic materials and processes, he is selling to ten or twelve Woolworth departments thousands of items every year. What to make is a constant problem. To solve it he asks: What do people want?

Mr. Rosenfield through all the depression years made money, and was remarkably free from labor troubles. In 1940 the product of which he was proudest was sun glasses, ground and polished. Made by old-fashioned methods they would cost, he said, about $10 a pair, but on chain-store counters (without the original price limit) the glasses could sell at not more than $1. At the same time he made frames for women's handbags, buttons, combs, hair ornaments, coasters, and hundreds of others things—all by a process of molding plastic raw material. In batteries of machines invented and made on his premises, the plastic, first ground to a crumblike form, becomes at intense heat fluid which may have any color he chooses. Under pressure this flows into a matrix of whatever shape is being made, and in response to a temperature change cools to solidity. The process is as simple as freezing ice cream into fanciful shapes; but the plastic, when "frozen," will melt again only at furnace heat.

And so, by playing ball with its manufacturers and when necessary guiding them along new paths, five-and-ten continued to boom despite its vexing war problems.

The steady increase of sales, the unyielding upward trend of profits, were a double tribute to the remarkable and specialized capacities of the five-and-ten executives. During 1914, fifty-three stores were opened; the year closed with 737 stores in the chain, and net sales were $69,619,669.

So bright was the picture that Woolworth buoyantly embarked on a $750,000 building operation of his own. He erected substantial mansions near his own for his daughters, Helena McCann and Jessie Donahue, and their families, purchasing for the purpose four old-fashioned houses at 4, 6, 8, and 10 East Eightieth street. Previously, a modern five-story residence at 2 East Eightieth street had been presented to the second daughter, Edna, and her husband, Franklyn Hutton. The group of family dwellings occupied a total frontage of 25.8 feet in Fifth Avenue and 250 feet in East Eightieth street.

There were now six Woolworth grandchildren. The three youngest, one in each family, had been born within six months of each other: Barbara Hutton, November 14, 1912; Woolworth Donahue, January 9, 1913; Helena Woolworth McCann, April 23, 1913. The other grandchildren were all little McCanns: Constance Woolworth, born November 7, 1905; Frazier Winfield, April 29, 1908; and Gladys Helena, June 1, 1910.

This merry batch of youngsters were the apples of their grandfather's eye and he wanted them grouped as closely about him as possible. Indeed, his social

life was confined almost entirely to his family and
small group of business associates.

With his annual European pilgrimages disrupted
by the war, Woolworth also acquired a handsome
estate at Glen Cove on the north shore of Long Island.
The house, with eighteen acres of lawn and wood-
land, commanded a splendid view of Long Island
Sound. Comfortable and roomy, it had been built in
1899 by Dr. Alexander Humphreys, who sold it to
Emmet Queen, a Pittsburgh banker. When Woolworth bought it from Mr. Queen, he installed a
$20,000 automatic organ and rechristened the place
Winfield Hall.

In the spring of 1915, death entered the ranks of
the pioneer five-and-ten men. Within three weeks
Carson C. Peck and Seymour H. Knox died.

For several years the universally loved Peck, con-
cealing his condition as best he could, had battled
valiantly against diabetes—contracted while, as candy
buyer, he consumed great quantities of sweets. Yet
the end came with comparative suddenness. On January 4 the office force tendered him a luncheon party
in honor of the twenty-fifth anniversary of his service
as general manager. Soon thereafter a scratch on the
forefinger of his right hand developed into blood
poisoning; and in March the finger was amputated.
The operation appeared successful and the patient
rallied immediately. Carrying the right arm in a sling,
but with eye clear and step firm, Peck attended a
meeting of the board of directors April 14; and moved
that the dividend on the common stock be increased
from 6 to 7 per cent, a motion which was carried.

A few days later there was a recurrence of physical
weakness, and Peck sank steadily until his death on
April 29. Shortly before the end he recovered con-

sciousness, spoke tenderly to his wife and two children, Clara and Fremont, and asked about the men at the office.

Woolworth, deeply affected, ordered all stores closed during the hour of the funeral and paid touching tribute to the "country boy" who had been his right bower for a quarter of a century.

Peck's interest in Brooklyn, where he had lived since his arrival in New York, led him, shortly before his death to purchase a newspaper, the *Brooklyn Daily Times*, which his son later ran for many years. The Carson C. Peck Memorial Hospital in Brooklyn, built and endowed by the family, perpetuates his memory.

Seymour Knox, one of the five founders of the F. W. Woolworth Company, died at his home in Buffalo on May 16, 1915. He had been in poor health for three years with kidney trouble and high blood pressure, and finally succumbed to uremic poisoning. He was but fifty-four years old. Besides a widow, formerly Grace Millard of Detroit, Knox was survived by a son, Seymour, Jr., and two daughters, Dorothy and Marjorie.

For many years Knox had been identified with practically every enterprise, civic and commercial, which forwarded the development of Buffalo. His sagacity and judgment were keenly valued. He had foraged successfully in many fields. Engineering a merger of the Marine National and the Columbia National banks, he served for a time as president of the enlarged institution. Other interests included railroads and lumber companies. In some of these investments, his friends Kirby and Charlton and his cousin Frank Woolworth participated.

Knox never lost his fondness for the farm and devoted much time to breeding horses and developing his Ideal stock farm at East Aurora, New York. He spent his summers on this farm, with its large racing stables and fast horses.

All Woolworth offices and stores were closed during the funeral; and Woolworth lauded Knox as "a prince among men," adding:

"We have lost two wonderful business men in Mr. Knox and Mr. Peck. But there are about ninety heads of different departments in the corporation and our business will go on. This is not a one man business any more than is the Standard Oil Company."

Peck had been treasurer as well as general manager, and also chairman of the executive committee. These posts were now divided. C. C. Griswold became general manager; Hubert T. Parson was elected treasurer; and Woolworth himself took over the executive committee chairmanship.

Charlie Griswold, the new first lieutenant, was as popular as Peck had been. A former farm boy and book agent, he had come up the ladder step by step since obtaining his first five-and-ten job in January, 1894, in the cellar stock room of the Albany, N. Y., store.

Griswold's first communication to the men in the field was a pep plea:

May 26, 1915: Be a better man and a better manager when your store closes at night than when you opened in the morning. Take pride in your work and get your help interested. Your janitor is a better janitor if you get him interested in his job; more so your clerks, your cashier, your assistant.

And his bulletins were pithy and to the point:

June, 1, 1915: WARNING—A Manager accused a lady of stealing in Dayton, Ohio, store. She sued the firm for $25,000; we defended the suit and won but the total charges we had to pay were $555.41. Wise man that bridles his tongue under provocation.

Under Griswold, each store was divided into thirty-two departments, with weekly and sometimes daily reports required from each: confectionery; baked goods; post cards; knitted goods; hosiery; millinery; laces; ribbons; handkerchiefs; towels; muslin goods; stamped goods; embroidery; jewelry; hair ornaments; stationery; notions; neckwear; music; novelties; tinware; glassware; toys; dolls; Japanese goods; pictures; woodenware; toilet articles; hardware; brushes; crockery; china.

The five-and-ten ran like a well-oiled machine. Many attempts were made to obtain information from gullible managers by outside individuals, presumably acting for rival chain stores. To thwart these activities, headquarters issued to those in authority identification cards which bore the signature and picture of the owner. The managers now knew to whom they could talk in confidence.

In 1915, despite war conditions, the number of stores grew to 805, a gain of sixty-eight for the year; and sales spurted to a new high of $75,995,774, with approximately a penny of profit on each ten-cent turnover.

Candy was by far the most remunerative item, a profit of no less than $3,347,000 being realized on total stales of $9,728,000. And, indicating careful attention to detail, the sum of $100,185.85 was cleared from the sale of waste paper, empty cases, candy pails, excelsior, etc.

The English stores were also flourishing, despite the war—their 1915 sales totaling more than $4,000,000. The general conscription act called fifty-two of the sixty-seven English managers to the colors. The parent American company immediately relieved this situation by supplying trained men from the American stores.

B. F. (Pop) Hunt, Woolworth's old friend, now over seventy, who had long represented the company in Germany, injected a personal note amid war's alarums:

Dear Mr. Woolworth:

I am here in Rotterdam with my wife. We were married in Leipzig on November 6. I have known the lady for some time and recently have had the opportunity to get better acquainted with her. When you come to Europe again, we shall be glad to have you visit us. With kindest regards,

B. F. Hunt.

This communication tickled the recipient beyond measure.

Despite occasional recurrent nervous attacks, Woolworth enjoyed to the full his prestige as a self-made magnate and owner of the world's tallest building. He attained membership in that sacred citadel of plutocracy, the Union League Club; frolicked with his fellow directors at "prosperity" parties staged with each gain of $1,000,000 in deposits by the Irving Bank; and often adorned a grand-tier box at the Metropolitan Opera House, which he leased for certain performances. This last affiliation, however, did not prevent his giving financial aid and comfort to the late Oscar Hammerstein in the picturesque impresario's independent operative ventures.

Occasionally the great man of the five-and-ten was persuaded into interviews, in which emerged such nuggets of wisdom as:

No man can make a success of a business which he does not like.

Dreaming never hurt anybody if he keeps working right behind the dream.

Never be afraid to run. If your business isn't going ahead right, back out and take a fresh start.

Pressed once for a "Success Code" for the budding business man, he obliged with the following, which today reads like a prime piece of Babbittry:

1—Of course you will be discouraged. But keep on.

2—If you believe in an idea, give it a chance. Some of my first stores failed because I placed them in the wrong part of town. There's always a right location. Find it.

3—Everybody likes to make a good bargain. Let him. Small profits on an article will become big profits if you sell enough of the articles.

4—I believe in doing business by and with cash. Large credit is a temptation to careless buying.

5—Supervise details but don't allow them to absorb you. Don't waste the time of a high-priced organizer on a clerk's job.

6—I prefer the boy from the farm to the college man. The college man won't begin at the bottom to learn the business.

7—There are plenty of opportunities today. Many young men fail because they are not will-

ing to sacrifice. No one ever built a business on
thoughts of having a good time.

As men often do when the years ripen, Woolworth
now displayed livelier interest in his boyhood sur-
roundings. At every opportunity he motored through
the North Country, revisited his birthplace, the farm
at Great Bend and familiar haunts in Watertown.
The returning pilgrim's purse was open to local char-
ities, but his main gift was a church in memory of
his parents.

The Woolworth Memorial Methodist Episcopal
Church of Great Bend was dedicated September 15,
1915; and the occasion was featured by an organ
recital, a banquet and much speech making and
merry making. The donor, his family and a party of
friends came to the celebration in a private railroad
car. In Great Bend he was greeted by Bishop Hamilton of Boston, District Superintendent Brown and
other dignitaries of the Methodist Church.

The pretty little edifice was crowded to capacity.
Presented with flowers by the inevitable bevy of little
girls in organdie, Woolworth was escorted to the platform; and delivered the following remarkable presen-
tation speech which has been preserved for posterity
because a young lady in the audience happened to be
practicing shorthand that day:

Ladies and gentlemen and friends of Great
Bend: You may ask the reason why I gave the
money for the construction of this church. There
is a reason. About one hundred and twenty-five
years ago this spot was in the midst of a wilder-
ness here. Pioneers came from New England and
Europe to settle on the land and to build their

homes. There was a necessity for a church and about one hundred years ago one was built about two miles south of there. I was asked why the church was built there, and my guess was that it was then the center of the settlement.

That church was not like the ones we have now. Many things in it were different. The pews had high backs so that when you sat down you could hardly see your neighbor in front of you. You could only see the tops of the heads. The pews were built this way so that the congregation could keep their eyes on the preacher. He was placed up high so that he had the drop on everyone in the church. I went to Sunday school in that church and they held Sunday school every Sunday. I had to learn seven verses of the lesson on the way to Sunday school. My parents thought that I was not getting enough church so they allowed me to go to the Baptist church here in the village, and I went there for a time.

This was a very good community, and I guess it's just as good now. I wanted to honor my father and mother, and for this reason I gave the community this church. My small part was to supply the dollars and cents. The greatest work devolved upon Mr. Brown, the two ministers and the trustees. Most of the credit should be given to them.

An unusual feature of the dedication of this property is that no collection will be made today. I have done all the collecting myself. The property, church and buildings, stand free and clear and I present to you, the trustees of the church, the deed to the property.

For the maintenance of the property I am not going to provide entirely. I know that you want to bear some of the expense, so I am now going to present to the secretary of the trustees an endowment of $20,000 in five per cent bonds for the maintenance of the church so that it will not become a burden on the congregation and the trustees. I hope that in time it may become too small for the congregation.

After the dedication ceremony, a church official attempted awkwardly to nail to the wall a framed copy of the terms of gift.

Woolworth stepped forward and with bold and accurate strokes drove the nail deep into the hard surface and hung the frame.

Soon such bold and accurate strokes, both mental and physical, diminished. For Woolworth's brief remaining years were blighted by ill health and tragedy.

Chapter XIV

Curtain

FRANK WOOLWORTH'S closing years, though crowned with continued commercial success, were clouded by personal misfortune. The most poignant tragedy was the failure of his wife's mind. Eventually Woolworth's own buoyant temperament flagged under the increasing pressure of strain and upset nerves.

In January, 1916, his chief lieutenant and general manager, C. C. Griswold, collapsed suddenly and was dead within a few days. Griswold's successor was none other than Hubert T. Parson, the former $8-a-week bookkeeper, who retained his post as treasurer and at the same time became vice chairman of the executive committee. J. F. Nutting, a Knox veteran, was also promoted to a vice-presidency and C. T. Newberry became superintendent of buyers.

Hardly had the new set-up begun to function when Woolworth was forced to bed with grippe; lying ill, but with a telephone at his bedside, he longed as never before for the peace and relaxation of pre-war Europe. As an alternative he decided to recuperate in a part of the country he had never seen—the Pacific Coast. He started out in early April, accompanied by Mr. and Mrs. Harry Albright and Miss Salter, the nurse who had been a member of the household since Woolworth's breakdown in 1912.

Though the trip did not benefit his health appreciably, it did temporarily raise his spirits. Everywhere he went—Los Angeles, San Francisco, Portland, Seattle—he was hailed as America's greatest retail merchant. "Welcome to Our President" banners flew from the five-and-tens and invitations were showered upon him, few of which his health permitted him to accept.

In Los Angeles, Woolworth renewed acquaintance with E. W. Barrett, whom he had not seen since the fall of 1875 when Barrett, head clerk of the Corner Store, had left Watertown with Golding to found a 99-cent emporium in Port Huron, Michigan—the venture that led, indirectly, to Woolworth's own entrance into the five-cent field.

"I want to thank you, Mr. Barrett, for your kindness to me when I came off the farm to work in the Corner Store," said Woolworth. "I remember you were getting the tremendous salary of $13 a week while I got just what I was worth—nothing."

"Well, Frank," replied Barrett, "at least you were not afraid of work and were willing to learn. But I can't get over how stout you have grown. I remember you as a mere sapling."

"I *was* just a sapling," laughed Woolworth, who now weighed 235 pounds.

Often Woolworth would try to slip into some of his stores incognito, but his trip was heralded with so much publicity that invariably he was recognized by employees who had seen his photograph in the papers. In Portland one vivacious salesgirl scribbled an extemporaneous poem on a piece of wrapping paper, which began: "When Mr. Woolworth comes to town, they make us all jump up and down."

However, the most amusing experience of the trip

took place in movieland. Visiting Universal City, the great motion picture center near Los Angeles, he was watching the filming of a ballroom scene when one of the directors persuaded him to go before the camera as a super.

"You are a gentleman who has mislaid his wife," explained the director. "Just walk across the room looking here and there for her and express concern when you can't find her."

Woolworth, in great glee, followed instructions to the letter. It was a high spot on his month's tour.

Delighted as he was with the Columbia River scenery and the views of Mt. Shasta and Mt. Hood, the enervating climate of the coast did not agree with Woolworth. Headaches and indigestion attacks increased and he remained in his berth, ill and exhausted, most of the way back East. However, sick as he was, he could not bear to forego stopping off at Watertown for the annual company meeting to be held May 17.

As usual, he wired W. H. Moore and was surprised when the latter did not meet him at the station. He had hardly settled in his rooms at the Woodruff Hotel when a messenger brought news that Mr. Moore had just died of a sudden stroke.

The news shook Woolworth to the core. For many years his first employer had been a sort of personal icon with him. Indeed, the old merchant's last act, that very morning, had been to arrange a luncheon in Woolworth's honor. The previous year Moore had suffered a slight stroke and had recently had most of his teeth removed. Woolworth attributed Moore's death to this fact; and thereafter resolutely refused dental care of his own teeth, which were chronically in bad condition.

While awaiting the funeral Woolworth arranged to

put up a six-story building on the site of the old Corner Store, now a five-and-ten—as a memorial to W. H. Moore.

Back in New York, in his Napoleonic office, Woolworth learned that 1916 sales were running far ahead of 1915. The avalanche of European war orders—billions upon billions of dollars worth—was putting gold pieces into pockets that had hitherto known only pennies, and the five-and-tens were garnering their share of the synthetic prosperity.

Rising costs were still the chief problem. This was combated through the organization's multiplied buying power, which yearly reached more enormous proportions. For example:

A certain gold-filled finger ring retailed at fifty cents. The Woolworth jewelry buyer told its manufacturer that he wanted this article for the five-and-tens to retail at a dime.

"Absurd!" snorted the manufacturer. "I can't make that ring so you can sell it at ten cents. Anyway, I am selling plenty as it is—more than four hundred and fifty dozen this year."

The Woolworth buyer laughed.

"Four hundred and fifty dozen!" he snorted in turn. "Why, that's just chicken feed. Make these rings for us at the right price and I'll use 60,000 dozen the first year. Enlarge your factory; we'll guarantee you against loss; and you'll make so much more money that it'll make your head swim."

The details were worked out. The rings were produced—genuine gold-filled rings—exactly the same as the fifty-cents ones. Woolworth sold them at ten cents. In 1916 the customers bought 6,000,000 of them.

Such merchandising wizardry, plus the general prosperity, helped pile up the 1916 sales to $87,189,-270—a gain of more than $11,000,000 over 1915. During the year 115 new stores were opened, bringing the total in the United States and Canada to 920.

Yearly incomes then were not a matter of public record, but Woolworth's individual share of the profits approximated $2,000,000. However, through the accident of fire, opportunity was soon given him to expend a sizable segment of his huge income.

On the afternoon of November 10, 1916, Woolworth stood and watched his stately stucco home at Glen Cove burn to the ground. Defective wiring in the top-floor billiard room was believed responsible and the flames were soon beyond control. The loss was $300,000.

"It's not the money," the five-and-ten magnate remarked sadly. "It's the fact that it's my home. I slept right up there last night," and he pointed to a charred and swaying girder marking the remains of a sleeping porch. The damage included destruction of a $20,000 organ, $75,000 worth of furniture and a fortune in rugs, pictures and bric-a-brac.

While the ashes were still warm, Woolworth was planning to rebuild. Not for social background but simply to satisfy his love of luxury, he wanted something more than a show place—a mansion of a richness and grandeur hitherto unknown. And he wanted it completed in time for his occupancy the following summer. It was. The new Winfield Hall, designed almost overnight by Cass Gilbert, was an imposing three-story Italian renaissance palace of white marble. Wired for sound, it contained among other features a $100,000 pipe organ with unique storm effects, the most elaborate ever installed in a private house, ten master bedrooms and fifteen servants' rooms. There was a garage for eighteen cars, with three housekeeping apartments, as well as six additional rooms and bath. There were two greenhouses.

Woolworth's growing fondness for marble again manifested itself.

In the main house, from the great hall, rose a wide marble staircase. Paneled walls of light colored blended marble extended to the second-story ceiling which was of ornamental plaster, highly gilded. The hall furniture was in walnut, chairs and sofas in crimson velvet with embroidery in gold. The drawing room was paneled in walnut, with rich ornamental plaster ceiling in color and gold; the library of French Gothic, with walnut woodwork and walls covered in rich fabric. The dining salon was eighteenth-century Georgian, the woodwork in small figured oak, the entire wall spaces covered with elaborate carving in lime wood after the manner of the famous eighteenth-century wood carver, Grinling Gibbons; the furniture was in antique gold, the seats and backs of the chairs in needlepoint. The breakfast room created an outdoor effect, with a clear glass ceiling, walls covered with lattice woodwork painted in pale green with growing vines and a fountain plashing in the center of a wall space. The billiard room was Georgian, its woodwork solid mahogany from floor to ceiling.

Woolworth's own suite on the second floor again reflected his admiration for Napoleon. His bedroom was in Empire style. Over the bed hung a canopy in red velvet with embroidery in gold, a copy of the canopy over the throne of Napoleon. The mahogany furniture and hangings were in deep yellow Empire damask. His sitting room was Elizabethan, paneled in oak, but the bathroom was an elaborate copy of one designed for Napoleon. It had mirrored walls framed by marble pilasters, a rich inlaid marble floor, fixtures cut from solid blocks of Siena marble. The metal work was in Empire style, highly ornamented, and finished in gold.

"My firm did the rooms of the second and third floors," says Helwig Schier, of Theo. Hofstatter & Company, Fifth Avenue decorators. "These bedrooms and bathrooms were the most elaborate our company has ever done; every detail was specially designed and passed on by Mr. Woolworth. The work in these rooms cost $200,000 and they were treated in ten different styles of architecture and decoration. We were ordered to go ahead when the architect's plans were accepted. I did the designing in the form of rough sketches while talking with Mr. Woolworth at his Fifth Avenue residence. He had very definite and positive ideas of his own. There were many meetings and most of them lasted well into the night.

"Making these drawings in his presence and following his every desire pleased Mr. Woolworth very much and made him feel that he was a big factor in the results obtained. When he occupied the house it gave him a lot of pleasure to show visitors the different rooms. He was so familiar with the details involved that it was like a lecture in architectural styles as he described them.

"The doors to the rooms had raised gold letters on the hall side in the lettering of the room's period. A guest staying overnight would be told that he would have the French Gothic, the Sheraton or the Louis XV room. It was all very unusual, but Mr. Woolworth wanted it that way."

All of these rooms were elaborately gilded and ornamented. In addition to those we have described there were:

Chinese writing room: In Chinese yellow and black and gold lacquer.

Chinese bedroom: In silver grey and old blue and gold lacquer.

Marie Antoinette bedroom: In old white and blue.

Sheraton room: In soft blue-green and fawn, satin-wood furniture with painted decorations.

French Gothic bedroom: In old stone color with antique gold, vaulted ceiling and stone mantel. Furniture in oak, seats covered in red and gold damask.

Italian bedroom: Walls in old white, ceiling in antique blue and gold, carved walnut doors. Walnut furniture; curtains in Vatican red velvet.

Louis XV room: Paneled wall in old ivory and antique gold; mural panels over all doors; hangings in rich brocade; furniture in woods with inlay.

Louis XIV bedroom: Painted paneled walls with mural decoration over all doors; hangings in rich brocade; furniture in French walnut and antique gold. This and most of the other bedrooms had specially designed and woven carpets of fine quality in colors to blend with the rooms.

With the completion of the Glen Cove residence, Woolworth developed an absorbing interest in decorating. In fact, it vied with music as a passion. Mr. Schier was called in to help remodel the Fifth Avenue mansion. The result was a marble entrance hall and staircase and a Gothic library—all on a par with the richness of the Glen Cove establishment.

Meanwhile the five-and-ten, despite America's entrance into the war with further economic disruption, was running like a well-synchronized machine. Sales for 1917 jumped to $98,102,857, and general manager Parson, by some actuarial method which he did not disclose, gave the number of customers as 891,844,155. There were 28,000 regular clerks, and many extra employees for special occasions.

Almost every item sold was coming direct from manufacturers. Of 1704 firms which the buyers had in active service, 1619 were manufacturers, 61 sales agents or importers, and only 24 jobbers. As against

88,182 packages of European goods imported in 1914, but 1438 packages were imported in 1917—principally laces from France and England. The search for substitutes had been successful. There was a stiff increase in Japanese imports; and buyers Harry Albright and J. S. Croll were sent to Japan in an effort to establish direct connections with manufacturers.

During the year chewing gum spurted into popularity, and over 10,000,000 packages were sold. Some 26,094 tons of candy brought in upward of $13,000,000. Other leading items: 100,000,000 post cards; 12,000,-000 pieces of knitted underwear; 7,878,000 yards of curtain goods; 7,450,024 finger rings and 1,659,312 earrings; 592,232,380 sheets of wax paper; 25,491,502 toys; 16,250,000 balls of crochet cotton; 18,000,000 pieces of enamelware.

Parson warned that goods would be difficult to obtain in 1918 and that changes might be sudden.

"If the war ends," he pointed out, "the buying public will stop, look and listen and wait for lower prices. So watch your stock and do not let it pile up. We don't want to be caught with big supplies or expensive merchandise."

Since the formation of the corporation an annual dinner was held, generally in January, for all executive and district office men. The hosts were usually one or more of the founders. At this function in 1918, Messrs. C. S. Woolworth, F. M. Kirby and E. P. Charlton passed out souvenir canes with silver ferules upon which were engraved: "1,000 Stores January 24, 1918."

Store Number 1,000 was erected on a site leased for twenty-one years at Fifth Avenue and Fortieth Street, New York, directly opposite the Public Library. The newspapers criticized rather freely this invasion of what had become the heart of New York's fashionable shopping district by a five-and-ten. Woolworth brushed the objections aside.

"The trouble is people in New York don't take a sufficiently broad view," he said impatiently. "They imagine that only the poorer classes patronize the five-and-ten-cent stores. That is no longer true. We have stores in other cities on the most exclusive, high-price streets and they are profitable. This one will pay too and Fifth Avenue will get used to us." It did.

For Woolworth, the spring of 1918 was heavy with tragedy.

On the morning of May 2 a maid, entering the bedroom of Woolworth's second daughter, Edna Hutton, found her dead. The Huttons, with their five-year-old daughter Barbara, were living temporarily at the Hotel Plaza. The city coroner certified that death was due to the ear ailment (Mastoiditis) from which she had long suffered. The hardened bones of the ear, the coroner declared, had caused severe contraction of the tongue muscles and consequent suffocation.

Edna Hutton was but thirty-five. A beautiful, sensitive, though at times morbid girl, she had been a favorite of her father; and she possessed a singing voice of almost concert caliber.

Mrs. Woolworth was unaware of her daughter's death. For, at sixty-three, Jennie Woolworth's mind had become permanently clouded. For some years her memory had been failing—then a definite deterioration became noticeable; and now, when she remembered her daughters at all, it was only as little children.

On June 7, 1918, Woolworth was forced to apply in the New York Supreme Court for a committee to care for the property of the wife to whom he had been married forty-two years. He took this action, the court was informed, to his "very great regret and sadness," adding that "it has become a necessity to report to the court that my wife is and has been for more than two years incompetent." Doctors George W. Jarman and William Moore Pritchard, in supporting petitions, said that Mrs. Woolworth's mind was almost a blank, a condition more common among persons of ninety or older. Mrs. Woolworth, it was set forth, owned the house at 209 Jefferson Avenue, Brooklyn; half interest in certain Philadelphia realty; and dower in her husband's property. The petition was granted.

Later in the year the family group was further saddened by the death of little eight-year-old Gladys Helena McCann. The baby of the third generation of six Woolworth grandchildren was now dimpled little Jimmy Donahue, born in June, 1915.

In his big, empty houses loneliness often gripped Woolworth. He sat at his organ control for hours. In the great dining rooms of the Fifth Avenue and Glen Cove residences, there were frequently but four persons at the table: Woolworth and his nurse, Miss Salter; the magnate's stricken wife and her attendant. No longer could he eat the heavier dishes that had once delighted him. For his teeth, which he had refused to have attended to since Moore's death, could only cope with softer foods. His favorite dish was overripe bananas.

Although Mrs. Woolworth seldom spoke and for the most part remained expressionless, now and then her face would light up when her husband would launch into his ready flow of anecdote and reminiscence. Sometimes he would talk of his ambitions, and one evening he remarked: "Do you know, I'd be happy if I could sell a watch for a dime, a watch that really worked and kept good time. I've talked the idea over for years with watchmakers in Switzerland and Germany. They all tell me it's quite impossible but I'm still not convinced." But mostly he was inclined to linger in the past. So much so that at times he was in the way of his fast-moving business organization.

Puttering around in his Napoleonic office, Woolworth sometimes fussed over trifles. He had a habit of pouncing upon minor mistakes or reminding his associates of past errors or episodes which they were quite willing to forget. The boys at the office, indeed, thoroughly approved of the decorating and building hobbies that kept the boss engaged at home.

One night the artful decorator, Schier, suggested that a man of Woolworth's eminence should not be content merely to live in a house on a modest Fifth Avenue corner. He should be master of a mansion occupying an entire square block—a palace fit for a pope, a king, a Doge of Venice, a Maharajah of India —yes, even Napoleon himself. Woolworth leaped at the idea and turned it over in his mind for months.

Other five-and-ten men had followed Woolworth's lead and Schier's firm received lucrative commissions from Fred Kirby, C. S. Woolworth and others. General manager Hubert Parson bought a residence at Fifth Avenue and Eighty-eighth Street and called upon Schier to remodel it, remarking: "I want everything to be richer and finer than the decorations in Mr. Woolworth's house." Woolworth laughed uproariously when he saw what Parson was trying to do.

Parson became so enveloped in the spirit of Woolworth grandeur that in 1918 he purchased as a country home for his wife and himself the large estate of Shadow Lawn in Elberon, New Jersey, which President Wilson had occupied as a summer White House. It was the beginning of a series of dizzy extravagances which eventually wrecked Parson's fortune and health.

"I will be blanmed for this," remarked Woolworth to Schier when he heard of the Shadow Lawn purchase. "It will be said that I gave this place to Parson."

Mr. Schier believed it quite possible that Woolworth had helped finance the purchase. For Parson was Woolworth's fair-haired boy, the son he had never had himself, and he was always eager to do something for him.

Indeed, his faith in Parson seemed justified. Despite the war handicaps of high prices and scarcity of labor, the five-and-ten business moved ahead with resistless momentum. In 1918, Parson's first full year in office, sales reached $107,175,749—a gain of $9,000,000 over 1917; though net earnings—$10,165,000—were proportionately a little lower. Dividends were paid on common and preferred stock and about $1,000,000 was added to surplus.

Into war service, either drafted or as volunteers, went 867 of the corporation's men, of whom 216 were managers, and twelve of them died. In the absence of these men, many of the older salesgirls took charge of stores. The work proved too strenuous for most of them and, with demobilization, they were glad to go back to their counters.

As the business flourished, Woolworth grew increasingly slothful, stouter and more indolent. The trays which he ordered placed in his serving pantry for a midnight "snack" groaned with soft, rich food. He refused to take any exercise, even a short walk. Occasionally he roused himself to send a personal message to the stores. One of them, telegraphed to each store with instructions to post on the employees' bulletin board, read: "Good morning. Did you say 'good morning' to each customer this morning? F. W. Woolworth." But, for the most part, his once keen interest in every detail of the great structure he had reared became blunted. Even personal matters were left largely in the hands of his capable secretary, Leroy Haynes.

Among extensive landscaping operations at Glen Cove a nine-hole golf course had been crowded in; but the master of Winfield Hall was indifferent. Although he still talked of building a block-square marble palace in New York, he did not talk convincingly. Instead, with what may have been prevision that his time was growing short, he ordered an elaborate mausoleum, with granite platform and bronze doors, in Woodlawn Cemetery to cost $100,000.

Superstitious dread, too, must have been a factor in his peculiar failure to execute a will superseding the brief document signed in 1889, before his first trip to Europe, in which he left all his property to his wife. After the legal declaration of Mrs. Woolworth's incompetency, Woolworth had his lawyer, William C. Breed, draw up another will in which the chief beneficiaries were his daughters. Ample provision was made for his wife's care and comfort; and trust funds, in equal amount, it is understood, were set up for each of his six grandchildren. In addition there were minor bequests to charity and to individuals.

Although he carried this second will about with him for weeks at a time, Woolworth could not bring himself to sign it. His pretext was that he had not made up his mind in the matter of certain minor codicils.

Woolworth's growing lassitude and toxicity were traced to his teeth, which he still refused to have treated. Though doctors warned him that septic poisoning would set in, he could not be dragged to a dentist's office. So pronounced did this phobia become that the sufferer would not permit anyone about him, including the doctors, to mention the subject.

The result was inevitable. He grew irritable. His barber, Fischer, and others who saw him daily noticed a wavering in his powers of concentration. He did not seem able to hold one subject in his mind for any length of time.

The last Sunday in March, 1919, Frank Taft, the organist, called on him: and Woolworth, lying on his Napoleonic bed, deplored the fact that America was not a musical nation like Germany and Italy. He said he had long thought of establishing a foundation to foster popular appreciation of fine music; but finally decided that this was properly a function of government. Did Taft think the government could be induced to establish a department of music, with headquarters in an imposing building in Washington? For two hours he talked of this and his love of music.

On Wednesday, April 2, Woolworth was at his office and received word from Parson, to his satisfaction, that sales were showing a healthy gain over the previous year.

Thursday he had a stenographer come up to his Fifth Avenue house to take care of an accumulation of personal correspondence. On Friday, April 4, he went to Glen Cove to spend the week-end.

When he arrived at Winfield Hall he complained of a sore throat and suffered a chill. He retired immediately after dinner and passed a restless night. All day Saturday and Saturday night he was in pain, with a high fever. However, his regular physician and Miss Salter were not alarmed until Sunday afternoon, when he became unconscious for two hours. A hasty consultation of physicians diagnosed the patient's ills as gallstones and uremic and septic poisoning, plus an infection of the throat which they considered only local.

Woolworth was given powerful purges and rallied

a little Sunday night. Monday morning he was strong enough to walk across the room, but in the afternoon he failed rapidly; lapsed into unconsciousness; and died at ten minutes before two A.M. Tuesday, April 8. He would have been sixty-seven on April 13.

His daughters, Mrs. McCann and Mrs. Donahue, and his brother were at the bedside. Son-in-law Franklyn Hutton and his daughter Barbara were in California.

The body was brought to New York and services held in the music room of the Fifth Avenue mansion on the morning of April 10. The house was a bower of floral tokens, and surviving Woolworth veterans came from near and far. Frank Taft played the organ, Mrs. Herbert Witherspoon sang; and prayers and brief tributes were delivered by Bishop Hamilton of the Methodist Episcopal Church, the Rev. Dr. S. Parkes Cadman and Rev. Smith W. Brown, formerly of Watertown. Pending completion of the Woolworth mausoleum, the body was placed in a private vault in Woodlawn Cemetery.

The Woolworth Company executive offices were closed from Tuesday until Friday; all district offices and stores were closed all day Thursday. During the hour of the funeral every wheel in the Woolworth building was stopped for five minutes, while tenants, employees and visitors stood with bared heads. S. S. Kresge, one of Woolworth's leading rivals in the low-price variety field, also closed his stores for an hour.

Editorial expression reflected the important and appealing figure Woolworth had grown to be in American mercantile life.

"Woolworth made his dreams come true by his grit and his faith in homely things and homely people," said the *New York Evening World.*

"He won a fortune," commented the *New York Sun,*

"not in showing how little could be sold for much, but how much could be sold for little."

"Woolworth's triumph was unique in the sense that he opened up to cultivation a seemingly barren field," observed the *Syracuse Herald;* and compared the dead man to other first-rank originators, inventors and producers stemming from upstate New York State: George Eastman, Philip Armour, and the Remingtons and Smith brothers of typewriter fame.

The family announced a few days after the funeral that bequests made in the unexecuted will to charitable institutions, relatives and employees would be carried out. Woolworth had never gone in for charity to any extent, but he had a private pension list which even today is quite lengthy.

The will, filed for probate in Mineola, Nassau County, Long Island, was the handwritten document of July 31, 1889, leaving everything to Mrs. Woolworth and making her the sole executor. Thus an incompetent woman, unaware of her husband's death, became one of the richest individuals in America.

Upon the death of Jennie Creighton Woolworth, which was not to come for five years, the estate would go, in equal proportion, to her legal heirs: Helena Woolworth McCann, Jessie Woolworth Donahue and Barbara Hutton, the chubby little six-year-old daughter of Edna Woolworth Hutton. Meanwhile the courts appointed as executors of the estate Mrs. Woolworth's two daughters, Mrs. McCann and Mrs. Donahue, and Hubert T. Parson.

Woolworth left personal property appraised at $29,916,337.90; and real estate valued at $874,666.66.

The net estate, deducting taxes, executors' commissions and other charges, totaled more than $27,000,000.

Woolworth owned more than twenty per cent of the common stock of the F. W. Woolworth Company—

107,164 shares out of 500,000. The common had earned $18.58 a share in 1918; and Woolworth's holdings were valued at $13,181,172.

He owned 18,975 of the 150,000 preferred shares in the Woolworth Company, valued at $2,201,100.

He owned the Woolworth Building practically outright, his equity being valued at $10,490,095.

Other assets included in the official appraisal were: Liberty Bonds $600,100; 1,794 shares in the Irvington National Bank and 879 in the Irving Trust Company, total valuation, $618,930; 945 shares in the Woolworth Building Safe Deposit Company, $165,373; shares in eleven railroad companies, $750,000; cash deposits in twelve banks, $155,834.

Winfield Hall was valued at $852,666; the Fifth Avenue house at $460,000. Personal effects at the former were set down at $127,832; at the latter, $221,093.55. His belongings in his private office in the Woolworth Building were appraised at $23,311.50. He had cigars worth $1,189.25 at the store of Benson & Hedges.

After his death the business structure which Frank Woolworth had reared rolled on to new heights of prosperity. And the fortune he left multiplied many fold.

The distribution of that fortune spells a story as fascinating as that of its accumulation.

Chapter XV

Aftermath

IN EVERYTHING except price, the Woolworth stores operate today exactly along the lines marked out by their founder.

The first price raise came in 1932 when a few articles were timidly displayed with tags bearing the revolutionary sum of twenty cents. But the spirit and romance of the old five and ten was shattered forever on November 13, 1935, at a meeting of the board of directors in their luxurious room on the twenty-fourth floor of the Woolworth skyscraper.

Here, in a chamber appropriate for nabobs of India, with its ornately gilded ceiling, richly damasked walls and heavily draped windows in shades of red, cherry, carmine; in a chamber designed by Frank Woolworth himself, in the colors identified with his stores in many lands, the five-and-ten directors assembled. There were twenty-four chairs at the table—1/6 gross according to the habitual reckoning processes of Woolworth-trained merchants.

Charles Sumner Woolworth, then seventy-nine, presided as chairman of the board. Two directors were women. They were Frank Woolworth's surviving daughters: Helena Woolworth McCann and Jessie

Woolworth Donahue. The third heiress, Barbara Hutton, daughter of the deceased Edna Woolworth Hutton, was not present—though she had come into personal control of her huge fortune two years before. There were many familiar faces: ex-President Hubert Parson, who had gotten his first job through a five cent want ad, his successor B. D. Miller, the former errand boy, grown gray and grizzled in the Woolworth service, and others. There were new faces, too, for Woolworth executives, like British admirals, start young and oblige each other to retire as they pass sixty. One of the newcomers was a quiet, round-faced man, Charles Wurtz Deyo, who in thirty years had come up from the basement of a small Canadian store to the position of vice president in charge of merchandise at New York headquarters.

Physically, the members of this assemblage were comfortable, but in their hearts, in their emotions, most of them were disturbed. For years they had religiously followed the five-and-ten founders' Mosaic dictum—nothing on a red front counter must ever be sold for more than ten cents. "Otherwise," Frank Woolworth had warned, not once but many times, "our stores will lose their charm for the public and we shall fail just as the ninety-nine cent store of my youth failed when it began to deal in multiples of ninety-nine cents."

It was not Woolworth, however, but these men and women gathered about the long table who had to face the problems of the 1930's.

In 1932, when the Hoover depression was approaching the doleful nadir which came later in the year, it was quiet, forceful Vice President Deyo (later to become president of the company) who championed the twenty-cent line of goods. Though most of the larger rival variety chains—Kress, Kresge, Newberry, Grant,

McCrory, etc., which in the aggregate now controlled almost as many stores as Woolworth—had long since raised their prices, the directors had been reluctant in their consent. But as prices plummeted, the hardboiled, experienced Woolworth buyers had been enabled to name their own figure on many new items which they had coveted for years. In the shake of lamb's tail, the twenty-cent goods had sold at the rate of a million dollars a month; and when, within a year the line had accounted for 15% of total sales, Brother Deyo trod the soft red carpets of the executive offices with a smile that reached from ear to ear.

In 1933 had come the New Deal and the NRA codes, which reduced hours and raised wages. The codes swelled the payroll by some $4,000,000 a year. Then, indeed, the twenty-cent line had become a life-line, but a life-line which soon needed strengthening. By 1935 it was evident that even the new limit was insufficient to combat rising costs. To set prices still higher was the purpose of the present meeting.

One of the directors formally recited: "Resolved, that the selling price limit of twenty cents on merchandise be discontinued."

Charles Sumner Woolworth gazed ahead. If his eyes wavered to the large imposing portrait against the wall at his left he was confronted by Brother Frank, whose blue eyes and white mustache might have seemed aquiver with resentment; a glance to the right met a portrait likeness of Seymour Knox; further down, lovable Carson Peck. The chairman's voice was scarcely audible in the clamor of "ayes." Thus five and ten, in its original guise, passed from the American scene, joining the oil cloth covered peddling pack, the country trader's chicken wagon, the dry goods store, and other relics of commerce.

So it was, nickel at a time, that Woolworth edged its price range upward. Today the tentative limit is one dollar and, though NRA died, the company has kept in line with the progressive thought of the period by maintaining at least the NRA standard of wages and hours for its 72,000 employees.

The new prices bring Woolworth into keener competition with important department stores. Also, the larger and bulkier goods handled require more space. Hence every dollar of surplus Woolworth cash is now going into the enlargement and improvement of existing stores rather than in the opening of new outlets. Indeed, when entering the streamlined, chromiumed emporiums on fashionable metropolitan thoroughfares, the shopper may wonder whether he and his dime have not strayed into the wrong place. Only five new stores were opened in 1938; only fourteen in 1939.

Since then, so far as new stores are concerned, there is indication that the saturation point has been reached. Yet the general picture continues bright, mainly because Woolworth operates as ever along the conservative, yet imaginative, lines laid down by the founder. The emphasis now is toward fewer, better, larger stores.

Woolworth conducts some 3,000 retail outlets in half a dozen countries, with more expected momentarily to join the chain. Following the 1912 merger, its stock, in a few years, appreciated twenty-fold.

The company marked down to $1 the $50,000,000 good-will item, retired all preferred stock and is still modestly capitalized. Of $200,000,000 stock authorized, only half had been issued up to 1940. Strictly speaking, Woolworth has remained a "family" affair and has never laid itself open to stock market speculation. Distribution of stock as issued is strictly regulated.

Year after year, the company ticks along like a well-ordered metronome. On the New York Stock Exchange the range of its stock fluctuations is conservatively narrow.

For many years after the merger, Woolworth stock, at nominal par value of $10, paid a dividend of $2.40. Sales in the United States, Canada and Cuba slowly and encouragingly mounted until they exceeded $300,000,000 annually. Net annual income averaged $30,000,000, of which more than $23,000,000 in dividends was regularly disbursed to 64,000 stockholders. Selling an average of 25 articles a year for every person in the three countries, Woolworth had 1,250,000,000 customers. There are many more patrons today, since the red fronts have recently become firmly entrenched in Mexico and, according to the commercial grapevine, are preparing an all-out invasion of Latin America.

In the spring of 1956, Mexico City shoppers got a new look at U. S. merchandising methods when Woolworth introduced the first of two new stores in the city, as a pilot project. Their almost immediate success led Woolworth to hasten plans for going into leading Mexican cities with as many as 27 stores, some of which have already been opened.

The Mexican venture has been trumpeted in business circles as betokening Woolworth's plans for a wholesale invasion of the widespread Latin American market. Although Woolworth officials are characteristically cautious, it is known that red fronts are scouting numerous possible locations in Spanish America.

The Mexican move was three years in the detailed planning stage. The toughest obstacle necessary to overcome was the stimulation of manufacture in Mexico itself of goods Woolworth could sell. The second problem lay in recruiting and training local help.

Within a few months, Mexican Woolworth triumphantly announced that 97 per cent of its 32,000 items were made in Mexico; even that some products were ready for export to the U. S. By 1957, the Mexican subsidiary was shipping handwoven Easter baskets to the U. S.

The personnel problem was met by training a dozen young Spanish-speaking junior executives in the Los Angeles area. These, together with nine Americans, established headquarters in Mexico City and recruited 300 young Mexicans as an initial sales force. Some of these spoke English as well as Spanish.

In the hope of making its trade name "Woolco" a "quality" asset, Mexican Woolworth made extra efforts to entice quality buyers. One result was that many manufacturers who, in the United States, wouldn't permit their products to go into a dime store, let down the bars for Mexican Woolworth. Nevertheless, three-quarters of the items offered there cost the customer less than $1 in Mexican currency.

Approximately one-third of Woolworth's profits flow from F. W. Woolworth & Co., Ltd., of England, in which the American company owns fifty-two per cent. British Woolworth has proved a true wonder child of international commerce. The venture, which Woolworth launched in Liverpool in 1909 over the objections of his men, expanded amazingly. In a few years it became a public subscription company, capitalized at 8,750,000 pounds, with 50,000 stockholders.

By the outbreak of World War II, British Woolworth operated 766 stores, dotting the British Isles from Stornaway on the north to the Island of Jersey on the south. For several years, until the war halted expansion, it opened new stores at the rate of one a week. Each unit returned an operating profit two to three times as large as its American counterpart. Despite heavier taxes, it yielded a net profit ($20,000,-000 in 1938, the year before the outbreak of World War II) approximating that of the American company.

Before war conditions scrambled everything, lush British Woolworth, in many respects, became the tail that wags the dog. In the cold calculations of the banker and broker, its market value actually exceeded U. S. Woolworth. These astute gentlemen placed total value of U. S. Woolworth at $446,000,000; British Woolworth at $465,000,000.

After the death of Fred M. Woolworth in 1923, British Woolworth, for almost three decades, was headed by W. L. Stephenson, the bright, energetic young man Frank Woolworth added to his staff in 1909. Stephenson became a multi-millionaire and one of England's outstanding merchant princes. Slim and trim in his sixties and later, he continued to be a dynamo of industry. Until World War II broke out, his favorite diversion was cruising aboard his magnificent yacht *Velsheda* (named for his daughters Velma, Sheila and Daphne) upon which he often entertained royalty.

Stephenson and Fred Woolworth coined great individual fortunes from British Woolworth. A lesser amount came to B. D. Miller, who returned to the United States in the early 1920's to become vice-president and treasurer of the American company. Fred Woolworth's only child Norman, short and stocky like his father, inherited his father's holdings. He, like the other Woolworth heirs, took no active part in the business. With his Canadian-born wife Pauline (Stanbury) Woolworth and their children, he long occupied an imposing mansion off Fifth Avenue, New York, with a summer estate in Maine.

Another foreign venture has not turned out so happily for Woolworth.

In the pre-Hitler Germany of 1927, the F. W. Woolworth Company, G.m.b.H., was launched with standardized prices of 25 and 50 pfennigs. It scored a quick success and, within a few years, 82 stores were operating in the principal cities of Germany. These proved a gold mine—but not for the parent company in New York. For Herr Hitler did not permit profits to flow to America. The Woolworth report for 1938 omitted from its income account the sum of $1,992,399.27 in unrealized dividends and undistributed earnings of the Germany company, with the wry observation that the omission was due to "continued foreign exchange restrictions."

This loss pulled U. S. Woolworth net income for 1938 down from the customary thirty millions plus to $28,584,000. However, the boys in New York reasoned that, should conditions change in Germany, the total value of the Woolworth enterprises could properly be computed at a billion dollars. Was there ever such a romance of nickels and dimes! (Conditions very soon did change in Germany—for the worse.)

And what of the human elements in this freshet of gold that came from the small coins of the proletariat?

None of the five founders of the original, modern Woolworth Company is living. The last survivors were Fred M. Kirby and C. S. Woolworth, the boyhood chums of the old Corner Store.

Kirby piled up more wealth than any of the five-and-ten men. Everything he touched turned to gold. He became one of America's leading philanthropists— his contributions to educational, religious, scientific and recreational groups and institutions had by 1940 reached the vast total of $68,000,000. But his mind failed and he waited the end in his splendid Georgian mansion high on an elevation in Glen Summit, near Wilkes-Barre, Pa.

C. S. Woolworth, until far into his eighties, became the only individual of the name who took active part in the management of the Woolworth Company. For many years before his death, this delightful, humorful old gentleman retained his post as alert chairman of the board, though by remote control.

In his final, semi-active years, C. S. Woolworth passed the winters in Palm Beach, the rest of the year in Scranton, Pa., where he and brother Frank had founded the second successful five-and-ten-cent store in 1880. The Scranton residence, modeled after the Metropolitan Club in New York, contained an organ, fine woodwork and a marble staircase with an iron balustrade, a reproduction of the one in the Petit Trianon at Versailles. However, the writer, who passed many rewarding hours with this hardy and companionable old gentleman, judged him happiest when pottering about his splendid farm near Scranton.

Frank Woolworth's fair-haired boy, Hubert Templeton Parson, the ex-bookkeeper, headed the company as president from 1919 until 1932.

As his fortune and prestige increased, he, too, became obsessed with ideas of Napoleonic grandeur. He ensconsed his wife and himself (there were no children) in a palatial residence on Fifth Avenue; acquired Shadow Lawn, once the summer White House on the New Jersey coast; and built an elaborate mansion in Avenue Foch, Paris.

Other five-and-ten nabobs had followed F. W. Woolworth's lead in lavish living, but none so extravagantly or with such disastrous results as Parson. When, in

1928, Shadow Lawn was destroyed by fire, Parson determined to erect upon its site a residence more sumptuous and showy than any Frank Woolworth had ever conceived. The furnishings and art work alone cost $3,000,000. From a huge main hall, sixty feet in height, opened great suites and galleries. It was undoubtedly one of the most striking show places of America. Into it, Parson poured practically his entire fortune. Then, when the Great Depression came along, Parson found himself buried under an avalanche of debts and mortgages, from which, his health wrecked, he sought unsuccessfully to extricate himself. The new Shadow Lawn remained a vast white elephant.

In 1932, Parson reached the retirement age of sixty. No effort was made to extend his term as president of the Woolworth Company. Instead, B. D. Miller was chosen to move into the Empire Room and, as president, wrestle with depression problems.

Three years later, Miller was succeeded by C. W. Deyo, originator of the twenty-cent line. Deyo's regime proved so satisfactory that, early in 1939, the retirement rule was waived by the board of directors so that he could continue in office.

At least a hundred men—buyers, heads of departments, managers, etc.—have become millionaires through their association with the five and ten. Harry Moody, Woolworth's chum of the Bushnell basement, left an estate inventoried at $5,307,165 when he died in 1925. C. P. Case, second man to be chosen as a lieutenant by Woolworth, was a multi-millionaire at his death on his Briarcliff Manor, N. Y., estate in 1937. Others of the Old Guard, including Alvin Ivie, C. B. Winslow and Edwin Merton McBrier, passed their declining years in travel or at useful hobbies—all handsome beneficiaries of the great five-and-ten bonanza.

Her mind still a blank, Woolworth's widow passed away at her Glen Cove home, May 21, 1924; and was buried beside him in Woodlawn Cemetery.

Jennie Creighton Woolworth outlived her husband by five years and forty-three days. If she had died forty-four days earlier, millions of dollars would have been saved in estate and inheritance taxes. Under the law, since she survived her husband by this brief period beyond five years, Mrs. Woolworth's estate was subject to additional Federal and State taxes, quite apart from the $8,000,000 levied after Woolworth's death. Thus, the merchant's failure to execute a will proved tremendously costly.

However, by 1924 the estate had tripled in value and the heirs—daughters Helena Woolworth McCann and Jessie Woolworth Donahue and the motherless little granddaughter Barbara Hutton, then eleven years old, came into some $25,000,000 each. The major portion of the inheritance was in Woolworth Company common stock. If the original Woolworth holdings in the common stock had been held intact from his death to, say, 1940, the total valuation, including returns from stock and cash dividends, could have been computed at $200,000,000.

In the interim, however, the millionheiresses disposed of a great deal of their holdings—just how much there is no way of telling. By 1940, an authoritative source expressed doubt whether the members of the immediate family, as of that time, "own as much as 15 per cent of the stock."

The three Woolworth heiresses were of contrasting types:

Mrs. McCann (baby Lena of the struggling Watertown days) was quiet and home-loving, her hobbies music and flowers. In her country home, Sunken Orchard, Oyster Bay, she raised prize-winning roses and a special variety of sweet pea; and personally tended them almost up to her death in 1938. Besides her husband, now dead also, Mrs. McCann was survived by a son and two daughters. One of the latter, Helena, became the wife of Winston Guest, well-known polo player.

Jessie Woolworth Donahue has had a more spectacular life. Blonde and slender, she is markedly generous and maintains estates in Palm Beach and Long Island, as well as a triplex apartment on Fifth Avenue. The apartment, it is interesting to note, has a marble staircase. Frank Woolworth's only surviving daughter is passionately fond of jewelry, particularly pearls and emeralds. One pearl necklace cost more than $600,000. Though she is said to possess some of the choicest specimens of jewels, she is not averse to adorning her person with baubles picked up in one of her father's stores.

Deeply in love with the dapper Irishman, James Paul Donahue, whom she married in 1912, she lavished gifts upon him. Their $50,000 private Pullman was named *Japauldon;* and their Southampton, L. I., villa, *Wooldon Manor.* Donahue, too, was open-handed and generous, though subject to spells of moodiness. During one of these, in 1931, at the age of forty-four, he killed himself by taking poison. This tragic event occurred in the mansion at 6 East Eightieth street given to the Donahues by Woolworth. Mrs. Donahue closed the house and has never returned to it.

There are two Donahue sons, Woolworth, forty, and James, thirty-eight. Neither has taken active interest in the Woolworth Company. In January, 1940, Woolworth Donahue married Mrs. Gretchen Wilson Hearst of Virginia, former wife of John Randolph Hearst and a great-granddaughter of Stonewall Jackson.

Mrs. Donahue and her sons are extremely popular

among the colony of wealthy and prominent Americans who pass the fashionable seasons along the Riviera or on Palm Beach's so-called Gold Coast. The McCanns, on the other hand, early established themselves in the older and more conservative Long Island social circle.

The third Woolworth heiress, Barbara Hutton, is one of the most publicized women in the world. Her share of the Woolworth fortune had grown to $40,000,000 by the time she came into outright possession on her twenty-first birthday, November 14, 1933. Even before that she had been widely headlined as America's Dollar Princess. A round, petulant little face that stared from the pages of countless newspapers and magazines was looked upon with envy by myriads; all America was familiar with her features, knew that she had an income of $2,000,000 a year because her grandfather had been the Dime Store King. And among those who became aware of the Woolworth heiress was a certain fantastic family of exiles living a hand-to-mouth existence in Paris: the Mdivanis.

Directed by the eldest sister, Nina, the five Mdivani children had their own scheme for getting on in the world. Under the Czar, the father, Zakhari Mdivani, had been a general of infantry, not a fashionable figure at court but always a provincial, stationed at Tiflis. His forebears, seemingly, had been Persians. There is no evidence that he had ever called himself Prince. But when the family reached Paris after the Bolshevik revolution with a swarm of other Russians, the mother (of Polish ancestry) registered herself at a police station as "Princess Mdivani." By that one act she arranged for the same life of ease for her children as had Frank Woolworth by his years of devotion to a business.

"Prince" Serge Mdivani and "Prince" David

Mdivani, strong, virile fellows, were hunting in the night clubs of Montmartre while their little brother Alexis was at home in their shabby Left Bank apartment washing the dishes. But none of the brothers was really wasting his marital opportunities. Finally, through the three Mdivani boys and their half dozen marriages to American women, newspaper readers became accustomed, but increasingly confused, by the title: "Princess Mdivani." Serge married Pola Negri and David, Mae Murray, both highly paid stars of Broadway and Hollywood. These relationships ended in divorces. Then Serge married Mary McCormic, the opera singer, and by the time she had divorced him, young Alexis was under way; he had married and been divorced by a Newport girl, Louise Van Alen. Thereafter the twice-divorced Serge married his youngest brother's grass widow and Alexis, free, proceeded to make the best marriage of the lot, to Barbara Hutton.

Barbara had been on a trip around the world when Alexis set out in pursuit. The first information Barbara's family had of the affair was when the American consul at Bangkok, Siam, put in a trans-oceanic telephone call to Franklyn Hutton informing him that his daughter was about to marry Alexis Mdivani.

Barbara, who had generously given $5,000,000 to her father when she came of age, settled $50,000 a year on her husband the day they were married. Thereafter to disciples of the society columns she became Princess Barbara, Princess "Babs" and then, after her Reno divorce, "Babs."

The day after her divorce from Mdivani in 1935, Barbara married Count Court Haugwitz Reventlow, a former German soldier of the first World War who had become a naturalized Dane. By him she had a son, her one and only child, who came into the world in London on February 24, 1936.

After divorcing Reventlow in 1938, Miss Hutton embarked on a dizzy merry-go-round of marriages, six in all, during the next twenty years. After the first two, subsequent husbands were actor Cary Grant, Prince Igor Troubetzkoy, Dominican diplomat Porfirio Rubirosa, and finally Baron von Cramm, noted German tennis virtuoso, whom she swore to love, cherish and obey in 1955.

So kaleidoscopic were the marriages, with attendant orgy of print and speculation, that one catty observer remarked that the young woman was beginning to take on a "slightly mildewed" appearance before her time.

Be that as it may, it is a fact that when Barbara's name is headlined in the newspapers some 3,000 managers of Woolworth stores shudder for their business. High executives reach for their telephones or cuss or writhe, according to their dispositions in moments of emotional stress.

The simple fact is that Frank Woolworth's best known grandchild is considered by those who run the business he made, decidedly not an asset. His name represents millions in good will, hers symbolizes extravagance. Eagerly they volunteer the information that long ago she disposed of most of her shares in F. W. Woolworth, which is a fact. Not all know that Princess Babs, with excellent guidance, has shrewdly invested in other fields, that her fortune is larger today than it ever was.

Actually, the little Countess, Princess, commoner is a warm-hearted person, kindly and wishing ill to no one. Even now, with all the arrows and ills which have beset her, there is about her an ethereal quality which few have sensed and understood. Her particular hobby is Oriental art. Once she surprised everybody in and out of society by privately publishing a slender volume of fragile and beautiful verse, reminiscent of the Chinese. The following are two examples:

BOWL OF JADE

I bring you my poor dreams
Caught in a green jade bowl
Carved untold years ago
Out of a Chinese soul.

RED ROSES ON A BOAT

Oh, were you only here with me
Their beauty to admire
How greater far their loveliness
My dreaming to inspire.

The Woolworth heiress' whole heart and soul are wrapped up in her son, Lance Reventlow. Destined to become one of the world's richest men, Lance is a very self-assured, very self-confident young man. When he turned twenty-one, on February 24, 1957, Lance's mother presented him with a $500,000 home perched high on a mountain in Beverly Hills, California, and came from Europe especially to attend the housewarming.

Lance is inordinately proud of his new home, which was designed to his specifications and has its own waterfall, a swimming pool which enters the living room, and a marble bath which holds 300 gallons of water.

An instrument panel with 36 buttons is at the head of his huge, fifteen-foot-square bed. By merely reaching out a finger, the young master is able to control the temperature of the house and the television and hi-fi sets in every room; it even has a button to start the water flowing in the bath.

The house is furnished in modern décor and the sliding glass windows in the living room command a matchless panorama of Los Angeles and environs. Burbling with enthusiasm, young Reventlow took Joe Hyams, the capable Hollywood reporter, on a tour of inspection and told him: "On a clear day I can see twenty-three miles out to the Pacific and on a really good day I can see San Diego, more than a hundred miles away."

The house overlooks Falcon's Lair, once occupied by the great screen lover, Rudolph Valentino. It now belongs to Doris Duke.

In the entire house there is but one oil painting, a portrait of his mother. It hangs in Lance's bedroom. Barbara tells him to remember the haunting look in the portrait's eyes when he too passionately pursues his principal hobby: racing his scarlet Maserati on speed tracks. Last winter he placed third in a race in Florida; and he hopes his mother soon will permit him to enter some of the crack European racing events. Thus far she has been adamantly against the idea.

Lance lives alone from choice and does his own cooking, although he has a part-time valet and all-round handy man in the person of an Englishman named Dudley Walker, who once served Cary Grant. Lance has no particular girl friend and, generally speaking, is wary of entanglements. He confided to Joe Hyams that one of the penalties of wealth is the suspicion it breeds that people might like him only for his money, not for himself. "I have to be constantly on the lookout to see if a girl is on the make for my money," he remarked.

Asked if he expected to come into a large inheritance, now that he has reached his legal majority,

Reventlow said: "No. I daresay mother will give me a block of stock or increase my allowance or something like that. It will be enough to enable me to go racing in Europe. So far I've been able to race only in America."

Lance cringes from talk about money and bristles if anything unkind is said about his mother. "All the publicity mother gets about her money and her husbands gives people the wrong idea about her. She inherited about $40,000,000 and I would guess she still has the same amount." Quite simply he added that he had miserable times in various boarding schools. "The kids were always kidding me about mother, her money and her marriages. That's the real reason my education stopped with high school.

"Money is such a nuisance," concluded the young man who may some day inherit a great segment of it.

Frank Woolworth's possessions have been scattered in many directions.

The Woolworth Building was sold to the Woolco Realty Corporation in 1924 to pay taxes and settle other estate obligations; and the famed Empire Room gradually became less Napoleonic in its furbishings.

The Fifth Avenue residence was torn down in 1925 and an apartment house erected upon its site. Its gorgeous household decorations, furniture and tapestries, rugs and objects of art had been sold previously under the auctioneer's hammer.

Winfield Hall, the white marble palace at Glen Cove, was sold in 1929 at a fraction of its cost to Robert S. Reynolds, who recently opened it to the public as a museum. Now tourists, for a fee, may view the glories that were once Woolworth's own.

Yet there is much left to remind the world of Frank Woolworth's career and achievements.

After a quarter-century, the Woolworth Building remains one of the world's superb structures, with a line of grace and countenance other skyscrapers have missed. Its eastern approach was made even more impressive in 1939 by the removal of the ancient and ugly Federal Building.

The Billion Dollar business he built from an improvised notions counter carries Woolworth's name to the corners of the earth.

These monuments promise to keep green the memory of one who was an extraordinary factor in the life of his time.

The End